The Russian Revolution

A Beginner's Guide

D0067051

ONEWORLD BEGINNER'S GUIDES combine an original, inventive, and engaging approach with expert analysis on subjects ranging from art and history to religion and politics, and everything in-between. Innovative and affordable, books in the series are perfect for anyone curious about the way the world works and the big ideas of our time.

aesthetics
africa
american politics
anarchism
animal behaviour
anthropology
anti-capitalism
aquinas
art
artificial intelligence
the bahai faith
the beat generation
the bible
biodiversity
bioterror & biowarfare
the brain
british politics
the Buddha
cancer
censorship
christianity
civil liberties
classical music
climate change
cloning
cold war
conservation
crimes against humanity
criminal psychology
critical thinking
daoism
democracy
descartes
dewey

dyslexia
energy
the enlightenment
engineering
epistemology
european union
evolution
evolutionary psychology
existentialism
fair trade
feminism
forensic science
french literature
french revolution
genetics
global terrorism
hinduism
history of science
homer
humanism
huxley
iran
islamic philosophy
islamic veil
journalism
judaism
lacan
life in the universe
literary theory
machiavelli
mafia & organized crime
magic
marx
medieval philosophy

middle east
modern slavery
NATO
the new testament
nietzsche
the northern ireland conflict
nutrition
oil
opera
the palestine–israeli conflict
particle physics
paul
philosophy
philosophy of mind
philosophy of religion
philosophy of science
planet earth
postmodernism
psychology
quantum physics
the qur'an
racism
reductionism
religion
renaissance art
the russian revolution
shakespeare
the small arms trade
sufism
the torah
united nations
volcanoes

Beginners
GUIDES

The Russian Revolution

A Beginner's Guide

Abraham Ascher

ONEWORLD

A Oneworld Paperback Original

First published in North America, Great Britain &
Australia by Oneworld Publications, 2014

ISBN 978-1-78074-387-5
eISBN 978-1-78074-388-2

Typeset by Siliconchips Services Ltd, UK
Cover design by vaguely memorable
Printed and bound in Denmark by
Nørhaven A/S

Oneworld Publications
10 Bloomsbury Street
London WC1B 3SR
England

A note on dates

Until January 1918, Russia retained the Julian calendar, which means that the dating of events appears to be thirteen days earlier than in the Western (Gregorian) calendar in use throughout most of Europe at the time. I use the Julian calendar for all events before 1918 and the Gregorian calendar thereafter.

Contents

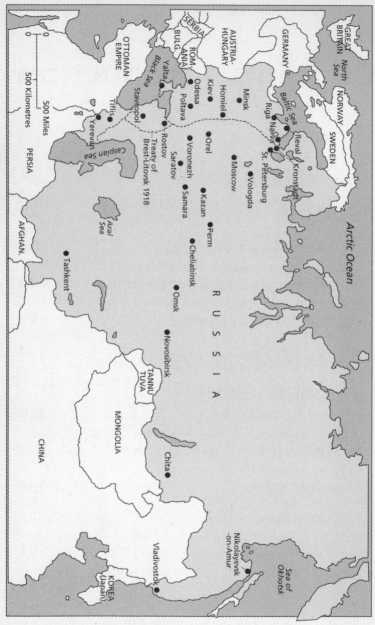

Russia, 1914

Introduction

In 1919, John Reed, a young American journalist fervently committed to socialism, published a stirring eye-witness account of the seizure of power by the Bolsheviks late in October 1917. Reed had traveled to Petrograd, the capital of the Russian Empire, in September that year to report on the progress of the revolution that had erupted in February and already toppled the authoritarian tsarist regime, leaving the country's political system in a state of uncertainty. The liberals who took control of the government were incapable of coping with the enormous problems they faced: the defeats the army was suffering at the hands of German troops in what seemed to be an endless war, the widespread industrial strikes, the peasants' unauthorized seizure of land, and the growing pressure of nationality groups to secure independence. Instead of bringing about a democratic and more just society, the dethronement of the unpopular Tsar Nicholas II had led to unprecedented economic, social, and political instability that threatened to thrust the Russian Empire into chaos.

Entranced by Vladimir I. Lenin and his followers, Reed was especially interested in reporting on their role in the dramatic events that were breaking the Russian Empire apart. If the Bolsheviks came to power, he believed, they would create an egalitarian order that would soon spread to Europe and eventually to the rest of the world. Moreover, the transformation of society in Russia would not be confined to the economic and social spheres; it would also be spiritual, in the deepest sense of the word. After attending the funeral of five hundred workers who had lost their lives in the revolutionary cause, he noted that 'I suddenly realized that the devout Russian people no longer needed priests to pray them into heaven. On earth they were building a kingdom more bright than any heaven had to offer, and for which it was a glory to die.'

Sensing the likely impact of the events he described on other countries, Reed titled his account, *Ten Days That Shook the World*. Lenin was so taken with the book that he 'unreservedly' recommended it 'to the workers of the world, who would gain from it a clear understanding of the "Proletarian Revolution and the Dictatorship of the Proletariat."'

Reed correctly stressed the importance of the turn of events in Russia, but he underestimated its eventual impact on world affairs. The upheaval in the Russian Empire shook the world not for ten days but for some seventy-four years. There was hardly a political development of significance in the twentieth century that was not profoundly affected by the Soviet Union, so great was the fear of Communism in many parts of the world. Had it not been for the dread of that political movement, it is highly unlikely that the Nazis would have become the largest political party in Germany and that Hitler would have been appointed Chancellor in 1933. Six years later, he plunged Europe into war and in 1941 attacked the Soviet Union, unleashing the bloodiest military conflict in human history. The Soviet Union emerged from that war as a major world power; it gained control of Eastern Europe and soon succeeded in producing nuclear weapons. Soviet leaders continued to speak of the inevitable triumph of socialism throughout the world, and they did their utmost to hasten it.

Western leaders, on the other hand, viewed that possibility as a threat to their societies and values, and spared no effort to keep Communism at bay. After World War II, when the Soviet Union emerged as a superpower, the struggle intensified and came to be known as the Cold War. That struggle between the West, led by the United States, and the Communist East dominated international relations from roughly 1948 until the collapse of the Soviet Union in 1991. It was a 'war' that in many ways shaped developments in Asia, the Middle East, Africa, and parts of Latin America. Nothing sums up the impact of Communism on the Western world more graphically than the quip by an American professor: 'If you tell me what a person's view of 1917 is, I can most probably divine his political views on all major contemporary issues.' Even a political analyst as perspicacious as Reed could not have foreseen that the seizure of power by a small group of radicals led by Lenin would so powerfully influence the course of history.

1

The road to revolution

The dream of an ideal society in Russia began to take shape in the 1880s, when a small group of Russian intellectuals founded a Marxist movement that claimed to represent the interests of the working class. Their leader, G. V. Plekhanov, contended that Russia's development would be similar to that of Central and Western Europe. The country would be industrialized and would then undergo a bourgeois revolution that would replace the autocratic system of rule with a constitutional order dominated by the middle class, which favored capitalism. Eventually, when industrialization reached maturity and the proletariat (the industrial working class) had become a powerful force, it would stage a second, socialist revolution, which had not yet taken place in Central and Western Europe. In 1898, the Russian Marxists formed the Russian Social Democratic Workers' Party, which five years later split into the Bolshevik and Menshevik factions.

Bolshevism

'Bolshevism' is the name of the Russian Marxist movement that emerged at the Second Congress of the Russian Social Democratic Party held in August 1903 in Brussels and London. The party split over what appeared to be a minor difference on how to define a party member. Vladimir Lenin, in his pamphlet *What Is to Be Done?*, written in 1902, had expressed his commitment to the creation of a highly centralized, elitist, and hierarchically structured political party. At the Congress, he defined a party member as anyone who 'recognized the party's program and supports it by material means and by personal participation in one of the party's organizations.' Lenin was aiming at the formation of a cadre of professional revolutionaries. Iulii Martov, however, wished to define a party member as anyone who supported the party 'by regular personal association under the direction of one of the party's organizations.' Martov and his followers, in other words, favored broad working-class participation in the movement's affairs and in the coming revolution. It also became evident that, although both factions subscribed to a revolutionary course, the Mensheviks tended to adopt more moderate tactics than the Bolsheviks.

Lenin's definition was adopted by a vote of twenty-eight to twenty-three; hence his faction adopted the name 'Bolsheviks', which means 'Majoritarians,' and Martov's supporters were stuck with the name 'Mensheviks,' which means 'Minoritarians.' This sobriquet put Martov's supporters at a disadvantage, even though on other issues they had sided with the majority.

Both groups continued to favor a revolutionary course to transform Russia into a socialist state, and the split did not become final until 1912. Even then, their basic aims continued to be identical, but in the ensuing struggle against the tsarist autocracy the Mensheviks tended to adopt more moderate positions than the Bolsheviks on whether or when to seize power and the economic and political policies to be imposed on Russia after the collapse of the Provisional Government in October 1917.

The Party of Socialist Revolutionaries (SRs), which were less doctrinaire than the Marxists but equally militant, claimed to speak for the peasants, who formed the vast majority of the population. The heirs of the populists of the 1870s, in 1901 the SRs formally created a political party committed to the idea that, since most people had been exposed to the egalitarian principles of the commune, the dominant institution in many regions of the country, the Russian Empire could attain socialism without passing through the stage of full-blown capitalism. The village commune, consisting of the elders of peasant households, handled the affairs of the local peasants; it tried peasants charged with minor crimes, it collected taxes, it decided on which youngsters would be recruited into the armed services, and, most importantly, it saw to the periodic distribution of land among its members to prevent wide differences in the holdings of individual families.

The SR Party advocated the transfer of all privately owned land to peasant communes or local associations, which in turn would assign it on an egalitarian basis to all who wished to earn their living by farming. Industry would be similarly socialized. Although the SRs insisted that the final goal, socialism, must be achieved by means of persuasion, they tolerated the 'Combat Organization,' an independent organ of the party that carried out dozens of political murders. Political terror, many SRs believed, was necessary to bring about the dismantling of the autocratic regime.

Liberalism emerged as an organized force in the late nineteenth century, when people associated with the *zemstvos*, institutions that exercised some powers of self-government on the local level, advocated extensive loosening of the autocratic system of government. They were joined in the late 1890s by a variety of middle-class citizens, such as lawyers, doctors, writers, and professors. These articulate intellectuals soon exerted an influence on the national scene far out of proportion to their numbers. Industrialists and businessmen in general were slower to take up the liberal cause; their economic dependence on the state made them politically cautious.

Zemstvo

In 1864, three years after the abolition of serfdom, the tsarist government established *zemstvos*, institutions of local government at the county (*uyezd*) and provincial levels in most regions of European Russia. The members of the new institutions were elected, but the electoral process was not democratic as we understand the word. The population was divided into three classes, or colleges: nobility, townsmen, and peasants. The number of representatives each could send to the zemstvos was based on the value of the property owned by each group. Moreover, the county zemstvos elected the delegates to the higher provincial zemstvo. As a result, nobles and government officials, a tiny minority of the population, played a decisive role in the organs of self-government.

Nonetheless, the zemstvos proved to be highly effective in initiating and overseeing the construction of new roads and in maintaining them, supervising local educational institutions, and sponsoring economic development, to mention some of their activities. In time, the zemstvos employed numerous experts such as doctors, agronomists, teachers, and engineers, who were referred to as the 'third element' and came to exercise considerable influence in local affairs. Early in the twentieth century, a fair number in this element, which now totaled about twenty thousand, showed strong sympathy for liberalism and socialism and often joined left-wing political movements. The zemstvos remained influential until the Bolshevik ascent to power late in 1917.

Like the Marxists, the liberals favored a fundamental reordering of society, but the two movements differed in their ultimate goals. The liberals advocated the rule of law, the granting of civil liberties to all citizens, a sharp curtailment of the powers of the monarch, the creation of a legislature elected by the people, and the maintenance of a capitalist economy. The journal they founded in 1902, *Osvobozhdenie* (Liberation) and their underground organization, the Union of Liberation, formed in 1904, helped mobilize public opinion against the old order and thus set the stage for the first Russian revolution.

Russia's backwardness

Given the economic, social and political backwardness of Russia, the proliferation of political parties, some favoring utopian goals and extremist tactics, is hardly surprising. At a time when much of Europe had turned to some form of popular participation in the political process, Russia continued to be an autocracy in which the Tsar claimed to rule by divine right. This claim was advanced with particular vigor by Nicholas II, who occupied the throne for twenty-three years (from 1894 until 1917), but proved to be singularly unfit to govern the country, as many people in high positions realized. On 19 October 1894, when it was clear that Tsar Alexander III was fatally ill, N. M. Chichaev, the Minister of War, trenchantly assessed the twenty-six-year-old Nicholas:

> The heir is a mere child, without experience, training, or even an inclination to study great problems of state. His interests are still those of a child, and it is impossible to predict what changes may be effected. At present, military service is the only subject that interests him. The helm of state is about to fall from the hands of an experienced mariner, and I fear that no hand like his is to grasp it for many years to come. What will be the course of the ship of state under these conditions the Lord only knows.

Nicholas's private letters and diary indicate that while he exuded personal charm, held strong religious convictions, and harbored deep affection for his wife and other members of his family, he showed no serious interest in politics. He took pains to describe evenings with his family and his various sporting activities, going so far as to note the number of birds he had bagged on his hunts. He could be deeply moved by events such as the loss of his favorite dog, Iman. 'I must confess,' he wrote on 20 October 1902, 'the whole day after it happened I never stopped crying—I still miss him dreadfully when I go for walks. He was such an intelligent, kind, and loyal dog!' Yet he devoted scant attention to the great events of his rule: the wars with Japan in 1904 and the Central Powers in 1914, the demands of liberals for a constitution, the industrial strikes, the Revolution of 1905, and the breakdown of public order that year.

Although moderately intelligent, Nicholas lacked the personal drive and vision to take charge of the government, to familiarize himself with the workings of the administration, and to instill a sense of purpose and direction in the ministers and bureaucrats. He was also narrow-minded and prejudiced, incapable of tolerating those who did not fit his conception of the true Russian. He especially disliked Jews and attributed his refusal to abolish restrictions on them to an 'inner voice' that told him it would be wrong to do so. Nor could he abide the intelligentsia. Once at a banquet when someone uttered the word 'intelligentsia,' he exploded: 'How repulsive I find that word.' He added, wistfully, that the Academy of Sciences ought to expunge the word from the Russian dictionary. Moreover, Nicholas firmly believed that all the people, except for the intelligentsia, the Jews, and the national minorities, were completely devoted to him.

In fact, a growing number of the population (of well over a hundred million) was becoming increasingly disgruntled. In the countryside, the peasants, who composed over 80 percent of Nicholas's subjects, chafed at the continued deterioration in economic conditions since their emancipation from serfdom in 1861. In the first place, the rapid growth in population between 1887 and 1905 resulted in a decline in the average landholding of peasant households of over 20 percent, from 13.2 to 10.4 *desiatinas* (one desiatina equals 2.7 acres). Productivity remained abysmally low, in large measure because the system of communal landownership, which governed about four-fifths of the peasants' holdings, was not conducive either to long-range planning or to the application of modern methods of farming. Many statistics could be cited to demonstrate the wretched conditions in the countryside, but none is more telling than the following: the Russian death rate was almost double that in England.

The government's fiscal policies also placed inordinate burdens on the peasantry. The expenses of the state treasury grew eightfold between 1861 and 1905, from 414,000 to 3.205 million rubles, necessitating new taxes, many of which were levied on consumer goods. Peasants had to pay these taxes in addition to the redemption dues that had been imposed on them at the time of emancipation. Unable to meet the tax bills, many poorer peasants were forced to sell their harvest in the fall, when plentiful supplies drove down prices. In the winter and spring, they would have to buy back some of the grain at exorbitant prices or take loans from landlords or *kulaks* (well-to-do peasants), which they would repay with labor if they lacked cash. For short-term loans, interest rates of 9.7 percent a month or 116.4 percent a year were not uncommon. If the peasant failed to make his payments, he might be subjected to whipping with a birch rod, or his property might be confiscated and sold. These measures did not have the desired effect. In the years from 1871 to 1875, the total peasant arrears in payments of various dues and taxes amounted to 29 million rubles. Twenty years later they totaled 119 million rubles.

The peasants were also forced to endure the heavy hand of bureaucracy. The emancipation of 1861 had freed them from serfdom and in 1864 they were given the right to participate in the election of zemstvos, although they chose far fewer representatives than the nobility. However, the peasants still could not move freely from one place to another and in numerous ways remained at the mercy of local landlords. During the reign of Alexander III (1881–94), the government enacted a series of counter-reforms that vastly increased the arbitrary power of local officials over the peasants. Most notably, provincial governors were charged with appointing land captains, who could overrule decisions of all local institutions, appoint personnel to important governmental positions, and, on their own authority, order the imprisonment of peasants for five days or impose five-ruble fines on them. Only in 1903 did the government prohibit corporal punishment of convicted criminals.

In view of these conditions in the countryside, the peasants' aloofness from revolutionary movements during the 1880s and 1890s may seem odd. However, organized political action could hardly have been expected from a social class that was geographically dispersed, cut off from urban centers of intellectual life, and still largely (over 80 percent) illiterate. On the other hand, in times of crisis the rural masses constituted yet another social group that sided with the forces opposing the prevailing order. Very often they erupted in elemental outbursts of anger at the authorities when unrest simmered in the towns.

Peasant unrest was not the only sign of social stress in the countryside. The *dvorianstvo* (nobility or gentry) was losing its grip economically and declining as a social and political force. Still, the nobles were unquestionably the main prop of the autocracy, even though they constituted a small and highly diverse group. According to the census of 1897, 1.5 percent of the population were either hereditary or lifetime nobles, among whom one could find, as the historian Hans Rogger put it:

> Rich … and poor ones, rustics and urbanites, reactionaries and liberals, capitalist operators of large estates, employers of hired or tenant labor (the majority of the landed gentry), rentiers, civil servants, officers, and professionals (one-fifth or more) who, at best, kept a tenuous foothold or summer home in the countryside. Half the nobility was non-Russian, and 28.6 percent who were Poles and discriminated against by the state hardly contributed to the solidarity of the class.

Even the ethnically Russian nobles were so diversified in their interests that they did not form a common political front. Although the majority ardently supported the autocracy, quite a few became active in the liberal movement, to the dismay of the Tsar and officials at court.

Although peasant unrest early in the twentieth century was a major factor in destabilizing the tsarist system of rule, the decisive social force behind the revolutionary turmoil turned out to be the industrial workers, a tiny portion of the total population that grew in size after the authorities decided, in the 1890s, that if Russia were to remain a significant player in the international arena it would have to embark on a program of rapid industrialization. However, they did not understand the implications of their decision. They deluded themselves into believing that they could modernize the country economically without altering the traditional social and political order.

The drive to industrialize

No one fostered this illusion more fervently than S. Iu. Witte, the brilliant architect of Russian industrialization who also played a central role in shaping government policies during the first fifteen months of the Revolution of 1905, the first major upheaval in the Russian Empire in the twentieth century. Witte quickly grasped the essentials of any problem he tackled and devised ingenious, if not always effective, solutions. He was masterly in judging the abilities of subordinates and in inducing them to do his bidding, but he was also fiercely ambitious, arrogant, cunning, and given to backstage intrigues. If he encountered obstacles he could not overcome, he lapsed into depression. Yet he always bounced back and pressed hard to implement his policies.

Witte advocated industrialization not because he believed that modernization was desirable in itself or because he wished to raise the standard of living of the Russian masses. He wanted to transform the economy primarily to bolster the political power and greatness of the state. It was this argument that appealed to

Tsar Alexander III, who appointed him Minister of Finance in 1892, and to Nicholas II, who retained him in that office until 1903. During those eleven years, Witte's achievements were, by virtually every standard, remarkable.

Count Witte

Count S. Iu. Witte was one of the two most eminent and gifted statesmen in late Imperial Russia (the other was Pyotr Stolypin) and his personality and career were probably the most colorful. Born in 1849 in Tiflis (now Tbilisi, Georgia), into a noble family, Witte aspired to a profession considered unsuitable for an aristocrat; he wanted to be professor of theoretical mathematics at the University of Novorossiisk, where he was an outstanding student. He was prevailed upon to abandon that goal and instead began training as an administrator in the railroads, a burgeoning field in Russia. In 1875, a wreck on the Odessa Railway, in which many lives were lost, endangered his career. He was held responsible for the disaster and sentenced to four months in prison. However, that very same Odessa railway was so successful in transporting soldiers and material during the Russo-Turkish war of 1877–8 that Grand Duke Nicholas Nikolaevich reduced his sentence to two weeks and allowed him to return to work.

His career then moved from one success to another. He was appointed Director of Railway Affairs in the Ministry of Finance, a post he occupied for eleven years, during which he initiated the first burst of industrialization. In 1903, Tsar Nicholas II appointed him Chairman of the Committee of Ministers, where he added two major accomplishments to his list of achievements: negotiating the peace treaty that concluded the conflict with Japan, from which Russia, the losing power, emerged relatively unscathed; and persuading Tsar Nicholas II to make extensive concessions to the opposition, which brought the general strike of October 1905 to an end.

Witte was not a liberal; on the contrary, he believed in the principle of autocracy, but he was also pragmatic enough to realize that some concessions had to be made to save as much as possible of the old order (government by an autocrat). His devotion to that order was so strong that he was willing to suffer personally from its rigidities. When his wife died in 1890, he married a divorcée who had converted to Orthodoxy from Judaism, each one of which was enough to make her unacceptable to high society. The tsarist court and many leading nobles were so shocked that Witte's wife was never invited to any social function at court. Despite the slight, Witte continued to serve his country.

Although some industries had been established by the 1880s, the real spurt occurred in the following decade, as a few statistics will indicate. In 1880, Russia had 22,865 kilometers of railway track. By 1890, almost 8,000 kilometers had been added, giving a total of 30,596; and by 1904 had virtually doubled, to 59,616 kilometers. Coal output in southern Russia jumped from 183 million *poods* in 1890 to 671 million poods in 1900 (1 pood equals 35.11 pounds). In the same region, the production of iron and steel rose from 8.6 million poods in 1890 to 75.8 million in 1900. Also in that decade, the production of cotton thread almost doubled and that of cloth increased by about two-thirds. By 1914, the Russian Empire was the fifth-largest industrial power in the world. However, in some important respects, economic progress was not as impressive as these figures suggest. Labor productivity and per capita income rose much more slowly than in Western Europe. In 1910, it amounted to only a third of the West European average, whereas in 1860 it had been slightly more than half.

Reliable statistics on the size of the industrial proletariat at the turn of the twentieth century are hard to find. The estimate of about three million in the late 1890s, made by M. I. Tugan-Baranovski, a respected Marxist scholar, appears to be reasonably accurate, which means that the proletariat constituted no more than 2.4 percent of the total population. No student of Russian history can fail to wonder how such a small proportion of the people came to exert so significant an influence on the political evolution of the empire.

To a large extent, the answer can be found in the peculiarities of Russia's industrialization. The country was a latecomer to the process, and the state played an inordinately large role in stimulating industrial development. Determined to press forward quickly, Witte launched an array of interrelated programs, the main purpose of which was to amass capital investment. Among other things, he promoted foreign loans and investment, established confidence in Russia's financial system by adopting the gold standard, placed extremely high tariffs on foreign industrial commodities, and substantially raised the rates of taxation. A large share of the financial burdens of these programs fell on low-income groups, especially the peasants, who had to pay high prices for manufactured goods and absorb the stiff indirect taxes on such items as tobacco, sugar, matches, and petroleum.

The state not only adopted policies to encourage industrial development but also participated directly in the nation's economy to an extent unequaled in any Western country. For example, in 1899, the state bought almost two-thirds of all metallurgical production. By the early twentieth century, it controlled some 70 percent of the railways. It also owned vast tracts of land, numerous mines and oilfields, and extensive forests. The national budgets from 1903 to 1913 indicate that the government received over 25 percent of its income from its various holdings. Thus, the economic well-being of private entrepreneurs depended in large measure on decisions of the authorities in St. Petersburg—a major reason for the political timidity of a substantial sector of the Russian middle class.

On the other hand, the concentration of industry, a result of the adoption of the forms of production and factory organization of more advanced countries, facilitated the emergence of a militant labor movement early in the process of industrialization. At the beginning of the twentieth century, Russia's manufacturing economy was more heavily concentrated than those of Germany and the United States, usually singled out as the pathfinders in this regard. For example, in 1866, 43 percent of the workers in the Russian cotton industry were employed at plants with more than one hundred employees; in 1877, 51 percent; in 1894, 72 percent. The existence of large factories was a boon to labor organizers and political activists, who could easily reach sizable numbers of workers resentful of the harsh conditions at the workplace.

The insensitive way senior government officials and industrialists handled the 'labor question' further fueled working-class militancy. Until 1905, they frequently asserted that there was no labor problem at all, that employers and their workers enjoyed a patriarchal relationship, comparable to the mutually beneficial relations between landlords and peasants. Consequently, they argued, the Russian worker, who was in any event less well educated than his counterpart in Western Europe and still tied to the land, would not succumb to the enticements of outside agitators, the alleged fomenters of labor unrest. Many officials knew that these assertions were baseless, but a frank acknowledgment by imperial authorities that the patriarchal relationship did not apply to the urban setting would have constituted, in the words of the historian Gaston V. Rimlinger, 'denial of the validity of the social order on which the tsarist regime was based.'

The disciplinary paternalism in industry, initially introduced by nobles who owned factories, grew harsher in the course of the nineteenth century, in part because the non-nobles who increasingly entered the entrepreneurial class lacked the tradition of *noblesse oblige*. The laws governing the contractual obligations of the worker were precise and stern, clearly designed to buttress the social and economic powers of the employer. Thus, amendments to the Penal Code in 1842 branded collective resistance to the employer as tantamount to an uprising against the state, punishable by fifteen to twenty years of hard labor. A strike for higher wages could result in prison sentences of three weeks to three months for instigators and seven days to three weeks for participants. In 1874, the Penal Code was further amended to make membership in an illegal organization that fomented strikes and unrest punishable by eight months' imprisonment in a fortress and exile to Siberia. During the next decade, the government issued several decrees that increased these penalties.

Conditions for factory workers were grim. After 1897, they normally worked eleven and a half hours a day for five days a week; somewhat less on Saturdays. They were paid poorly, and since many (the exact numbers are in dispute) returned for part of the year to their villages to work in the fields, they were housed in large, unsanitary barracks during their service at the factory. Industrialists, the historian Gaston V. Rimlinger noted, often acted like 'Tsars in their realm' and looked upon their workers 'as servants and slaves.' The employers and their managers were condescending to the laborers, addressing them by the familiar 'thou,' searching them for stolen goods at the end of the workday, and imposing fines on them for infractions of the intricate 'rules of internal order.' Any act of insubordination was punishable by a fine.

The wide cultural gulf between workers on the one hand and factory supervisors and government officials on the other exacerbated relations between them. In 1897, about 50 percent of the proletariat was illiterate, and many who were classed as literate could only barely read and write. That workers were not only economically exploited but also profoundly humiliated goes a long way to explaining why they frequently gave vent to rage during periods of revolutionary turbulence.

In the meantime, it had become apparent that Russian workers would not permanently accept their status of inferiority and remain docile. Between 1862 and 1869, six strikes and twenty-nine 'disturbances' took place; from 1870 to 1885 the average number of annual strikes rose to twenty and the number of disturbances from three to seventy-three. Some of the strikes, such as those in the St. Petersburg cotton mills in 1870, Kreenholm in Narva, Estonia in 1872, and Orekhovo-Zuevo near Moscow in 1885, were so massive as to suggest a significant change in the proletariat's mood. Even some government officials began to acknowledge publicly that labor strife, far from simply being perpetrated by outside agitators, was actually rooted in working conditions. By 1884, the police in St. Petersburg and Moscow, who kept an eye on all potential sources of disorder, had issued several reports on the erosion of the paternalistic relationship between manufacturer and employee. The police contended that masters paid their workers too little, showed no concern for their well-being, and had lost their respect. The social ideals propagated by the tsarist regime were manifestly not being implemented in the industrial sector of the economy.

On the initiative of an enlightened Minister of Finance, N. Kh. Bunge, a child labor law was adopted in 1882, which prohibited the employment of children under twelve, limited the workday of youngsters aged twelve to fifteen to eight hours, and placed restrictions on the use of children for night work. Inspectors employed by the government to enforce the legislation performed half-heartedly and were seen by many workers as often caring more about the employers' profits than the employees' well-being.

In 1899, the government adopted new measures to prevent strikes. The Third Department of the Ministry of Internal Affairs established an elaborate network of police surveillance in industrial enterprises, ostensibly for the purpose of studying such matters as the economic life of the factories and workers' conditions. Instead, the police devoted much of their time to ferreting out the instigators of strikes and arresting them before strikes could occur. Discovering the leaders of a potential strike, however, was not easy. Indeed, labor unrest continued to rise rapidly, as official figures indicate: between 1886 and 1894, the annual average was thirty-three; between 1895 and 1904, 176. During the massive strikes of 1896 and 1897 in the textile mills of St. Petersburg, workers revealed an unprecedented degree of sophistication, unity, and discipline. There could no longer be any doubt about the Russian workers' ability to act forcefully to advance their interests. The strike movement reached its highest level in the period before the Revolution of 1905 in 1903, when 138,877 workers staged 550 stoppages. The one policy that might have defused labor unrest, the legalization of independent unions and strikes, was never tried, because the government feared that it would undermine the entire structure of autocratic rule.

Early in the twentieth century, then, three principal issues motivated the opposition to the old order in Russia. The first was the constitutional question: How could the anachronistic political structure of the empire be altered to introduce civil liberties and assure a redistribution of power? The second was the labor question: How could the demands of the industrial proletariat for improvement in its social and economic conditions be met? The third was the agrarian question: How could the land hunger of millions of peasants be satisfied? The liberals, workers, and peasants constituted fairly distinct social groups, each of which emphasized one of the three issues, but by the spring of 1905 their agitation overlapped, which set off an unprecedented social and political crisis. The government could restore political stability only if it addressed the aspirations of these three protest movements, a state of affairs the authorities found disagreeable, both because they were reluctant to make any concessions at all and because they faced conflicting demands from various sectors of the opposition.

To complicate matters further, the national aspirations of minorities also provoked discontent, though most were not sufficiently aroused by this issue to pose a serious problem for the authorities until 1917, but even during the first revolution in 1905 those sentiments served to exacerbate tensions in various parts of the country.

Russification

The Russian Empire, the accretion of centuries of colonization, military conquest, and annexation of weak principalities by

Muscovite rulers, comprised over a hundred ethnic groups with a range of cultures, languages, and religions. The Great Russians, who made up less than half the country's population—somewhat over 44 percent according to the census of 1897—claimed to be the dominant group and exerted a paramount influence in politics, occupying most of the important positions in the bureaucracy and military services. By the late nineteenth century, the authorities in St. Petersburg made plain their determination to preserve the hegemony of the Great Russians and even to increase their influence by reducing to a minimum the cultural and political autonomy of the minorities. The last two rulers, Tsars Alexander III and Nicholas II, embarked on a policy of ruthless Russification, partly for reasons of security. Concentrated in the borderlands, the minorities were looked upon as a potential danger in times of war. In addition, the tsars feared that the special rights and privileges, cultural as well as political, enjoyed by some of the nationalities (notably the Finns and, to a much lesser degree, the Poles) would serve as a model for other minorities, among whom national consciousness was beginning to take root. If autonomy were widely extended, the empire would cease to be a 'unitary state,' to use the parlance of the time, and the autocrat's power would be sharply curtailed.

The authorities in St. Petersburg were also motivated by sheer prejudice. They considered the minorities to be culturally inferior, and were especially antagonistic toward the Jews, who numbered about five million. The government imposed economic, legal, and social restrictions on the Jews that were more extensive and demeaning than the measures against any other group. Forced, with few exceptions, to live in one region in the western and southwestern provinces, known as the Pale of Settlement, Jews also had to pay special taxes, could not attain the rank of officer in the army, and were almost completely excluded from employment in the bureaucracy. Moreover, their attendance at secondary schools and institutions of higher learning was constrained by quotas. At bottom, the hostility toward the Jews derived from the belief that they were marked by 'inner vices' that made their full assimilation into Russian society impossible. The prominence of Jews in all the radical movements and, to a lesser extent, in the liberal movement was in large measure the fruit of the government's discriminatory policies.

Although the entire opposition condemned the government's policies of Russification and oppression of minorities, it did not adopt a uniform stand on the national question, which further complicated the struggle between the advocates of change and the champions of the *status quo*. The radicals favored either full autonomy or self-determination for the minorities, whereas many liberals opposed the decentralization of political authority, a stand that antagonized some minority groups, especially the Polish nationalists. The liberals generally believed that a constitutional government in St. Petersburg that respected cultural differences would retain the loyalty of all the empire's subjects regardless of their national identity. In light of the growing force of nationalism, liberals seem to have been deluding themselves.

War with Japan

Domestic discontents in Imperial Russia were numerous and deep, but by themselves did not generate mass uprisings threatening the foundations of the state. In 1905, as in 1917, popular upheavals erupted at a time when political leaders had blundered into military conflicts that were badly managed and had led to catastrophic defeats. Only when the Tsar and his advisers proved to be incompetent as well as heartless did the people challenge the authorities *en masse*. In neither instance did the military conflict make revolution inevitable, but it created the preconditions for rebellion.

Although it has never been proved that the Russian government deliberately provoked Japan to divert attention from domestic tensions, there is little doubt that some senior officials mindlessly pursued a foreign policy in the Far East that was bound to be viewed with alarm by Japan. Russia began to abandon its generally cautious policy in the Pacific region in the 1890s, in response to Japan's emergence as a strong, aggressive power, and China's weakness. Eager to promote the country's economic development, the authorities in St. Petersburg adopted various measures to extend Russia's influence over two regions also coveted by Japan: Manchuria, which was part of China, and Korea, an autonomous kingdom under the suzerainty of the Chinese Emperor. At the same time, the Russian government decided to construct the Trans-Siberian Railroad. Finance Minister Witte was interested primarily in the economic exploitation of the area, which was rich in resources and markets, and he made it clear that he favored a cautious foreign policy that would avoid needless provocation of other powers. Russian diplomats, however, adopted an assertive, imprudent stance toward Japan and on several occasions during the 1890s forced Japan to abandon positions on the mainland. According to the historian John A. White, these humiliations evoked a 'paroxysm of public indignation' among the Japanese, who embarked on a program of rapid expansion of their armed forces.

Early in the twentieth century, tensions between the two powers reached a climax. Japan had vastly increased its economic and political influence over Korea, whereas Russia had extended its influence over neighboring Manchuria. When a Russian speculator, A. M. Bezobrazov, received a concession from the Korean government to cut timber on the Yalu and Tumen rivers, the Japanese government became alarmed. To calm the waters, it proposed an arrangement whereby Russia would be granted predominance in Manchuria in return for Japan's predominance in Korea. The Russian government dawdled, and in January 1904 the Japanese pressed St. Petersburg for a speedy reply. When none was forthcoming, they decided on a course of action they had believed for some time to be inevitable. On 26 January, they launched a surprise attack on Russian ships at Port Arthur and Chemulpo, a foretaste of what happened thirty-seven years later, when the Japanese attacked the United States naval base at Pearl Harbor, in Hawaii, also without warning, bringing America into World War II.

Although surprised and indignant at Japan's treachery, the Tsar, his advisers and the public at large were not particularly apprehensive. Everyone at the tsarist court thought that Russia faced a minor inconvenience and that the Japanese 'adventure' would be quickly 'terminated.' The liberal press, most notably *Russkie vedomosti* and *Vestnik Evropy*, referred to Russia's 'historical destiny' to advance in the Far East and to the necessity of protecting the country against an aggressive and unscrupulous enemy. It was widely believed that Russia's resources were so much greater than Japan's that victory was assured. Among the revolutionary Left, the war attracted surprisingly little attention, although the leaders did denounce the government's adventurism.

The optimism did not last long. Soon after hostilities began, it became clear that Japan enjoyed enormous advantages. Its troops and naval forces were better trained, its intelligence services were more effective, and, unlike Russia, it did not face the formidable task of having to transport reinforcements almost 4,400 miles over a still-primitive railway system. Russia suffered one humiliating defeat after another, at sea and on land, and public enthusiasm for the war quickly evaporated.

The Russians' most dramatic setback came in May 1905, when a large fleet commanded by Admiral Z. P. Rozhdestvensky arrived in the Far East with orders to engage the Japanese navy. As soon as the fleet of eight battleships, twelve cruisers, and various auxiliary ships reached the Straits of Tsushima, it encountered the Japanese fleet, commanded by Admiral Togo Heihachiro. In size, the two fleets were about evenly matched, but Togo's intelligence included detailed information about the location and movements of the Russian ships, and his forces were well rested. Battle was joined early in the afternoon of 14 May 1905, and within forty-five minutes the Russian navy suffered a devastating defeat. All told, the Japanese destroyed twenty-one Russian ships and captured four battleships and two hospital ships. Six Russian ships escaped to neutral ports, where they were disarmed, and only four reached Vladivostok. With this triumph, Japan gained undisputed mastery over the Pacific.

On land, the Russians fared no better, sustaining one humiliating defeat after another. A key factor was the poor showing of the officers, many of whom tended to be confused once their troops faced the enemy; they often took flight rather than encourage their troops. Even before the spring of 1905, when the worst military disasters befell Russia, the mood of Russian society had begun to sour. As early as the spring of 1904, newspapers had abandoned their optimism. Initially, they simply expressed shock at Russia's inability to defeat Japan quickly, but soon their comments became much sharper. The moderate Prince S. N. Trubetskoi, who in January had strongly supported the war, now argued that 'Russia could survive only if her government agreed to reforms.'

More than military humiliation generated opposition to the war. The war debilitated the economy, which was in the early stages of recovery after a prolonged slump. Usually, wars tend to stimulate economic activity, but the decision to transport only military goods on the Trans-Siberian Railway adversely affected some important sectors of the national economy. The production of silk goods, for example, declined by over 25 percent in 1904, that of woolen goods by about 15 percent, and that of cotton goods, chemicals, and some other industrial products by a smaller, but nevertheless significant, percentage. In addition, the call to arms of about 1.2 million reservists, often the most productive workers, reduced output in the handicraft industries. Unemployment rose sharply and the local organs of government that were charged with providing charity to indigent families found it increasingly difficult to fulfill this obligation. Many such families received much less help than they needed.

The change in the public mood became most noticeable in the summer of 1904 when a terrorist assassinated V. K. Plehve, the reactionary Minister of Internal Affairs. The response of people in various strata of society to the elimination of the most dynamic and most intransigent figure in the government exposed the depth of despair over the state of affairs. The new mood was captured by Count Aloys Lexa von Aehrenthal, the Austro-Hungarian Ambassador to St. Petersburg. In a report to Vienna, he noted that although one could not expect much sympathy for so 'authoritarian' a person as Plehve, one could have expected: '... a certain degree of human compassion, or at least concern and anxiety with respect to the immediate future ... [of the country]. Up to now I have found only totally indifferent people or people so cynical that they say that no other outcome was to be expected.'

2

1905: dress rehearsal for 1917?

Many citizens now began to question not only the wisdom of waging war against Japan but also the legitimacy of the entire political system. In the autumn and winter of 1904–5, the liberals, who had held their tongues so long as the government's policies seemed to be widely supported, unleashed the so-called 'banquet campaign' for fundamental constitutional changes. It was astonishingly effective and marked the beginning of a nationwide assault on the autocracy that lasted two and a half years. As the historian Terence Emmons pointed out, the events, modeled on the famous banquets in Paris of 1847–8, were intended to unite the intelligentsia 'around the constitutional banner.' The organizers urged liberals throughout the country to hold banquets in honor of the fortieth anniversary of the judicial reforms. The authorities were invariably reluctant to permit the meetings, but in the end they relented, on the understanding that all the gatherings would be 'private.'

The rash of political meetings that ensued—thirty-eight in twenty-six cities—was unprecedented in Russian history. Zemstvo activists were the most prominent participants, but some local bureaucrats, nobles, journalists, and teachers also took part. The banquets adopted various kinds of resolutions, but to one degree or another all contributed to mobilizing support for the demands of the liberals. Although the banquets were private affairs, several major newspapers described most of them in detail, thus publicizing the demands of the opposition. These meetings, it should be noted, were held at a time of considerable unrest in the country: a growing number of strikes by workers, a series of pogroms aimed at Jews, and several assassinations of officials.

In response to the campaign, P. D. Sviatopolk–Mirsky, the Minister of Internal Affairs, urged the Tsar to take the bold step of establishing an institution composed of elected deputies that would participate in legislative work. Nicholas was not interested and turned for advice to Witte, who opposed any far-reaching constitutional changes. On hearing the news of the Tsar's decision, Mirsky lost heart. 'Everything has failed,' he said to some colleagues. 'Let's build jails.' Support for the beleaguered authorities within society dwindled dramatically, and for that reason alone, Nicholas's decision to follow Witte's advice to reject reform must be classed among the most critical of his reign. Liberals warned the government that failure to introduce basic reforms would further enrage the opposition.

The Gapon effect

The liberals had in mind the impact of the banquet campaign on worker-activists. A fair number were impressed by the outpouring of petitions, which they read with great interest and which prompted them to consider producing their own appeals. Even more importantly, a leader of the St. Petersburg workers at this time and a key figure in the unfolding of the revolution, Father Georgii Apollonovich Gapon, established contact with several members of the local branch of the Union of Liberation, who supplied him with newspapers and information on the liberal movement. Actually, Gapon, who was as charismatic as he was enigmatic, had already created an impressive organization of workers. The US ambassador to St. Petersburg considered him to be a 'thoroughpaced revolutionary' who 'utterly deceived' workers into believing he had their interests at heart. Count Aehrenthal, the Austrian ambassador to Russia, claimed that the 'Jewish press' had elevated him to the level of a 'historical figure,' whereas in reality he was a degenerate who had violated a twelve-year-old girl. Still others viewed him as nothing but a toady of the tsarist police. About the only judgment on Gapon on which his associates, contemporary observers, and historians can agree is that he had a magnetic personality and was instrumental in triggering the second—and most turbulent and violent—phase of the revolution. Handsome, intelligent, and articulate, he impressed acquaintances with his dedication to humane principles and loyalty to his associates. He was a fine speaker, and, when it served his interests, could be crafty and duplicitous.

Gapon had turned to public service as a student at the Poltava Seminary. He came to have doubts about the Orthodox Church's emphasis on ritual and its 'religious formalism,' which led him to abandon religious work and to devote himself to improving the lot of 'the toiling and suffering masses.' Gapon's organizational skills were outstanding; early in the summer of 1902 he began to lay the groundwork for a political movement that would become a significant force within two years. As a loyal supporter of the autocracy and the government, he set out to steer workers along a path acceptable to the authorities and to employers. His plan fitted almost perfectly with the effort of the government to take the lead in organizing industrial workers to secure better conditions in return for their political loyalty to the tsarist regime. This effort, known as police socialism or *Zubatovshchina*, was the brainchild of Sergei Zubatov, a police officer and an ardent admirer of tsarism—so much so that when Nicholas II abdicated in 1917, he committed suicide. In 1901, Zubatov formed the first police union and within two years a sizable number of workers had joined the movement.

Although Gapon disapproved of Zubatov's stress on tight police control over the workers' unions, the two men agreed to collaborate. Even after Zubatov was ousted from his position as a result of intrigues against him, Gapon continued with his own projects regarding workers. Supplied by the government with a monthly subsidy of a hundred rubles (a substantial sum at the time), Gapon founded the Assembly of the Russian Factory and Mill Workers of the City of St. Petersburg in the summer of 1903. It carefully avoided involvement in labor disputes, concentrating instead on organizing dances, concerts, and lectures, and on promoting various projects for self-improvement. Gapon deliberately restricted himself to activities that were politically innocuous because he planned eventually to expand the organization, in both the capital and other cities, and wanted to avoid any action that might appear provocative or threatening to the authorities. He was amazingly successful, and by January 1905 his organization in the capital had a membership estimated at 20,000. Although workers under the influence of revolutionary movements distrusted him, there is no question, as an article in the journal *Byloe* (The Past) noted in 1906, that he had 'cast a spell' over a large number of ordinary laborers and that his adherents were prepared to 'march with him through fire and water.'

Early in January 1905, workers at the Putilov Plant in St. Petersburg, a large armaments and shipbuilding factory, decided to go on strike to protest against the arbitrary dismissal of four of their colleagues. Realizing that the mood of the public had turned toward militancy, Gapon was now prepared to reveal his support for fundamental political change. He endorsed the strike and also began feverish preparations for a large procession to be held on Sunday, 9 January, to present the Tsar with a list of proposals for reform. On one day alone, he delivered fifty short speeches to workers, always exuding unbounded confidence in his plans. Generally, he told his audiences that the Tsar was a good man who would help the people once he understood their plight, but occasionally he acknowledged the possibility of failure, in which case it would be evident that 'we have no Tsar.'

The Bolsheviks and Mensheviks disapproved of the procession, on the grounds that the petition to be presented to the Tsar did not sufficiently stress political demands. In fact, Gapon had given every assurance to the authorities that the procession would be peaceful, but officials nevertheless feared the worst. The people responded enthusiastically to Gapon's appeal, and early on 9 January somewhere between fifty and a hundred thousand appeared, dressed in their Sunday best, at designated places. Many women and children showed up, and all participated in prayer meetings held before the procession began. Marchers carried icons and portraits of the Tsar and sang 'Save Thy People, O Lord.' Many pointedly raised their hands and emptied their pockets to show that they were unarmed. Their goal was to reach the Winter Palace, the Tsar's residence, and to hand the petition to the ruler himself.

Although the petition was moderate in tone, its demands were far-reaching. It called for a constituent assembly elected on the basis of democratic suffrage, civil liberties for all subjects, equality of all before the law, the right to establish trade unions, and an eight-hour working day. It is worth emphasizing that the petition did not demand the abolition of the monarchy or the introduction of socialism. Nor did it contain threats of violence.

The authorities, however, took no chances. Troops were brought in from various regions to reinforce the local garrison, and by the appointed day about nine thousand infantrymen and three thousand cavalrymen were held in readiness in the capital. There is no evidence that the Tsar and his advisers wanted a violent confrontation, but they had made two operational decisions that made a clash unavoidable: first, not to grant Gapon a meeting with the Tsar to present the petition, and second, not to permit marching workers to enter the center of the city. Beyond that, there was no clear-cut plan to be followed by the troops.

As the marchers approached the center of the city, soldiers in a few places ordered them to turn back, but no one paid heed. When one large crowd, which included Gapon, who was surrounded by a protective shield of workers, reached the Narva Gate, a bugle was blown as a signal to the soldiers to open fire. It is not known who ordered the resort to violence to force the marchers to retreat. Gapon escaped injury, but two of his bodyguards and an official of the Assembly died on the spot. Several other bodyguards threw Gapon over a fence, and for several days he hid in different private apartments, including that of the writer Maxim Gorky. Enraged by the violence, Gapon exclaimed, 'There is no God any longer! There is no Tsar!'

Shooting then erupted at other places and in the afternoon shots were fired at crowds that had gathered in the Winter Palace Square. When the carnage ended, some 130 people had been killed and 299 seriously wounded. The day immediately became known as 'Bloody Sunday' and is generally considered to have marked the beginning of the Revolution of 1905. For orthodox Marxists, the events of that year did not actually amount to a revolution, because political power was not transferred from one class to another. Non-Marxists, who define a revolution as a fundamental change in the system of legality, might also hesitate to use the term because the Tsar's authority remained paramount, even though it was clearly reduced.

Yet there are good reasons for the adoption of the term by contemporaries and for its retention by political activists as well as historians. From late 1904 until late 1905, the assault on authority from below was so massive, potent, and successful that the old regime appeared to be disintegrating. The challenge to the established order came from mass movements representing several social groups: liberals among the middle class and nobility, industrial workers, peasants, and some of the national minorities. In addition, by this time many landlords and factory owners had lost confidence in the Tsar. The ultimate aims of these groups differed in fundamental ways, but they were united in their determination to end autocratic rule in Russia, which they all held responsible for the country's economic stagnation and archaic social and political institutions. In addition, considerable unrest and numerous mutinies disrupted the army and navy. Virtually no geographical region remained unaffected by the turbulence. Moreover, the currents of rebellion were so diverse that at times it seemed as though Russia was undergoing not one revolution but a series of parallel revolutions. Civil order broke down, and for several months the government seemed capable of doing little more than biding its time until the outbursts of defiance, generally unplanned and unorganized, had spent themselves. So effective a challenge to the state's monopoly of power, even though temporary, may justifiably be characterized as a revolution.

The changes that swept over the Russian Empire would have been unthinkable two years before Bloody Sunday. Newspapers now regularly ignored long-standing restrictions by printing what editors believed the public should know, and the government, in effect acknowledging its impotence, largely ignored infractions of regulations that had been on the books for decades. Readers were informed in vivid detail of disorders in the cities and countryside, the clamor for basic reform, the military disasters Russia had suffered at the hands of Japan, and of discussions by opponents of the autocracy on how to change the country's institutions. On several occasions, confidential deliberations of senior bureaucrats or official committees were leaked to the press, which readily ran articles about them. The liberal newspaper *Russkie vedomosti* frequently denounced the incompetence and arbitrariness of the 'disgraceful ... bureaucratic system' and asserted that nothing short of a constitutional system with civil liberties guaranteed to all subjects would restore order and stability. In May 1905, the newspaper echoed the by-now-popular cry of liberals: 'We can no longer live like this.'

Unrest in the countryside

Other signs of governmental weakness surfaced. The authorities failed to maintain order during the rash of attacks on innocent civilians by hooligans and right-wing extremists, known as the Black Hundreds, that broke out shortly after Bloody Sunday in many cities and towns. Pogroms against Jews in a wide area of the empire were an especially virulent form of disorder that the authorities failed to stop. The labor unrest that swept across the country in 1905 was unprecedented in its magnitude and thrust. None of the previous strikes had touched as explicitly, directly, and frequently on political issues, and officials soon gave up trying to enforce the law against work stoppages.

Workers scored some notable victories: in 70 percent of the so-called economic strikes, workers won partial or complete victories. In mid-May 1905, during a strike in Ivanovo-Voznesensk, an organization emerged that should be mentioned because of its subsequent importance in Russian history: the *soviet* (council). The initial purpose of this elected body was to provide workers with unified leadership and to serve as a strike committee, but gradually, as soviets sprang up in over forty cities, many assumed leadership roles in struggles for economic and political change.

Soviet

The word '*soviet*', which translates as 'council', was widely used in tsarist Russia to describe political organizations such as the 'Council of Ministers'. During the Revolution of 1905, the word assumed a more specific meaning: in May that year, a 'Council of Workers' Deputies' was elected by workers in Ivanovo-Voznesensk to represent their interests during a strike. By the time of the general strike in October 1905, soviets had been formed in numerous other cities in the Russian Empire, the most influential being in the capital, St. Petersburg. The soviets still represented the economic interests of their constituents, but by this time had also become active and influential in local and national political affairs. In the course of 1917, a rash of Soviets of Workers' and Soldiers' Deputies were elected, and once again the St. Petersburg soviet became the most prominent. Until mid-September 1917, the representatives of the Socialist Revolutionaries and the Mensheviks were considerably more numerous than those of the Bolsheviks, but after the attempt of counterrevolutionaries to overthrow the Provisional Government late that summer, the Bolsheviks won a majority in the capital's soviet. At that point, Lenin began to call for a Bolshevik seizure of power and the establishment of a political order based on the soviets. In 1922, the country was officially designated as the Union of Soviet Socialist Republics.

The assault on authority was especially virulent in several border-lands of the empire, the Polish kingdom, the Baltic provinces, and Guriia, a small, picturesque area in western Georgia bordering on the Black Sea and Turkey (where unrest had started in 1903, long before the outbreak of revolution in St. Petersburg). The disturbances in these three regions were characterized by two features: they were notably violent from the start, and they acquired an explicitly political thrust earlier than the mass protest movements in the ethnically Russian regions of the country.

Tsarist officials who remained optimistic about the regime's ability to survive the protests counted on the docility of the peasants. This is surprising, since historically, unrest in the countryside was by no means uncommon. However, many officials labored under the illusion that the peasants' loyalty to the Tsar, their 'little father,' was so deep that they would not join the revolution. In fact, unrest in the countryside in 1905 became intense; according to reliable estimates, more than three thousand disturbances involving peasants occurred throughout the empire. Generally, peasants of all socioeconomic levels took part, and, perhaps surprisingly, the poorest peasants and agricultural laborers, who could not survive without their daily earnings, were often the most restrained. The unrest took various forms and differed from region to region. Some of the more popular forms of rebellion involved the felling of trees and seizure of lumber, strikes by agricultural workers, seizure of meadows and pastures, and conflicts over rent between tenants and landlords. The authorities ruthlessly applied force to stop the unrest. Police and soldiers would swoop down on villages to search for stolen goods, and offenders were flogged mercilessly. In one village in Chernigov Province, a group of peasants was forced to kneel in the snow for hours, after which they were whipped. Often, haphazardly established military courts handed down quick and severe sentences on those who had engaged in illegal actions or had submitted demands to landlords accompanied by threats of violence.

Ultimately, the fate of the autocracy depended on the loyalty of the country's military forces. If large numbers had refused to obey orders, if they had gone over to the side of the striking workers, rebellious peasants, or minority groups in the borderlands, the autocratic regime would not have survived. On numerous occasions, soldiers and sailors refused orders to put down the uprisings, and in some instances actually joined the opposition. At such times, senior officials experienced some anxious moments but in the end most soldiers remained loyal to the regime and carried out orders to crush the opposition.

The revolution triumphant

The high point of the assault on authority was reached in October 1905, when the opposition succeeded in bringing the government to its knees and in securing far-reaching political concessions that remained in force until 1917. The key event was the general strike that no one expected and no one had planned.

As is often the case at times of political and social tension, one particular dispute, for reasons hard to explain, serves as a spark for a massive outbreak of protests. In 1905, that spark was a dispute between railway workers and their employers that resulted in a strike involving thousands of workers. To boost their chances of success, the leaders of the railway workers called for a general strike to begin on 4 October. Within a few days, the strike spread throughout Moscow and soon broke out in many other cities. Two weeks later, work stoppages were reported in virtually every city in the Empire; all told, over two million workers and white-collar employees left their jobs. In the capital, mass meetings at the University of St. Petersburg, totaling about thirty thousand people, unanimously adopted a resolution to join the all-Russia railway strike, and within the next few days industrial workers, telegraph operators, salesmen and pharmacists, and employees of private banks, government offices and city utilities failed to show up for work. University students, as well as high school students, stopped attending class. Even the Imperial Theater, private theaters, and the Mariinskii Ballet closed their doors. Food stores opened for only three hours a day. The empire was paralyzed. Deprived of many vital services, people believed, according to the newspaper *Vestnik Evropy*, that they were 'experiencing the predicament of Robinson Crusoe.'

Initially, the political Left was caught unawares and a fair number of the most ardent supporters of revolution remained diffident about the mass action. The Moscow Bolsheviks, distrustful of any action not directed at a seizure of power, failed to declare their support for the general strike until 10 October, and the St. Petersburg Bolsheviks waited even longer, until the night of 12 October.

Aside from a few incidents of violence and scattered attempts by strikers to intimidate colleagues who refused to leave their jobs, the general strike was in many ways an extraordinary event, remarkable for the high degree of discipline and self-sacrifice shown by masses of people. It is no exaggeration to say that in October 1905 the industrial proletariat emerged as an organized—and the most dynamic—force in the revolution. It initiated the strike, kept it going, and provided most of the cannon fodder for the assault on the old order. The workers probably could not have succeeded in bringing the government to its knees without the support of white-collar employees, professionals, and the middle class, but if the workers had not taken the lead, there would have been no general strike in the first place. In the nine months since Bloody Sunday, the proletariat had undergone a notable degree of politicization, and the autocracy's failure to introduce fundamental reforms had induced a decisive shift to the Left in society. The congruence of these two developments furnished the essential backdrop to the general strike, the opposition's most impressive challenge to the autocracy during the revolution.

During the general strike, the soviets became a powerful voice of the proletariat. They appeared spontaneously, elected by the workers, sometimes rather haphazardly, and quickly evolved into a force that the authorities could not ignore. In a few localities, they assumed some of the functions of the government.

The tsarist government was at a loss as to how to deal with the strike. At first, General D. F. Trepov, the Governor-General of St. Petersburg, announced that he had ordered the police and army to put down all disturbances with the 'most decisive measures,' and that they had been advised 'not to use blanks [or] to spare bullets.' The intimidation did not work. On the very day the proclamation was distributed, some forty thousand people defiantly streamed into the streets near the university. In addition, every auditorium in the main building was filled to capacity with men and women from various labor unions. However, the army and police were nowhere to be seen. The authorities realized that any attempt to disperse the crowd would lead to a bloodbath more terrible than that of 9 January.

Several advisers to the Tsar concluded that only political reform could bring the crisis to an end. The main spokesman of this group was Witte, who had recently returned from the Japanese peace negotiations—which had ended on 23 August—with a greatly enhanced reputation because he had managed, despite Russia's defeat, to conclude the conflict on much better terms than Russia could have hoped for. Reluctantly, the Tsar agreed to let Witte deal with the crisis, even though the former Minister of Finance believed that in view of the continuing unrest, major concessions to the political opposition would be necessary. The reform Witte had in mind was an imperial manifesto granting civil and political rights to the people and providing for the establishment of a 'unified ministry' headed by a prime minister who would have primary responsibility for running the government, an arrangement that would reduce the powers of the ruler. Witte was confident that his plan would detach the moderates from the opposition and that he could count on the loyalty of the peasants to the Tsar, and consequently he would be able to return the country to an even keel.

Witte warned Nicholas that if he failed to adopt his strategy he would have to appoint a dictator who would act in the name of the Tsar and would be empowered to subdue the opposition by force. Such a course, Witte believed, would spare the Tsar from being blamed for the use of force. After extensive discussion with his advisers, Nicholas indicated partial acceptance of Witte's program, the creation of a 'unified ministry,' but Witte insisted that this measure alone would not end the turbulence. Nicholas called another meeting of advisers, including his cousin, Grand Duke Nikolai Nikolaevich, the only person with the necessary qualifications for the post of dictator: he was a zealous defender of the autocracy, who enjoyed the confidence of the sovereign and the good graces of the imperial family. However, Nikolai Nikolaevich had reached the conclusion that there was no acceptable alternative to political reform, and only after a dramatic meeting between him and Nicholas did the latter finally decide, on 17 October, to accept Witte's proposal.

According to Witte, when Count Frederiks, the Minister of the Court, informed the Grand Duke that the Tsar wanted him to take over as dictator, the following scene was played out: 'The Grand Duke took a revolver from his pocket: "You see this revolver," he said, "I am now going to the Tsar and will implore him to sign the manifesto and Witte's program; either he signs or I will shoot myself."' Only then did the sovereign agree to sign the Manifesto.

The brief Manifesto of 17 October was basically an outline of reforms the government intended to introduce in the coming months. It would grant such civil liberties as personal inviolability, freedom of conscience, speech, and assembly and the right of association, and promised that in the future no measure would become law without the approval of an elected state *Duma* (parliament). The last point was critical, for by conceding that he was no longer the sole repository of political power, Nicholas did what he had vowed never to do: he abandoned the principle of autocracy. A principal demand of the opposition appeared to have been granted.

Within days, most workers, who were beginning to suffer great hardships, returned to their jobs, even though it was not clear what powers the Tsar retained. It soon turned out that he retained a veto over all legislation, maintained control over foreign affairs, and still commanded the armed services. On the other hand, vast numbers of people were now politicized and activists formed three new parties, two of which were to play a key role in national affairs over the following decade, when a primary issue was the consolidation of Russia's transition from monarchical rule to representative government. During a congress held on 21–8 October 1905, liberals formed the Constitutional Democratic Party for People's Freedom, generally known as the Kadets. It favored a political system that would assign primacy to an elected legislature rather than the monarch.

The Constitutional Democrats

The Constitutional Democratic Party (also known as the *Kadets*) was founded in mid-October 1905 at a time when Russia was in the throes of a general strike that prompted Tsar Nicholas II to make several concessions to the opposition, principally the holding of elections to a parliament (*Duma*, from the Russian 'to think'), whose approval would be required for all laws. In theory, at least, Nicholas had abandoned the principle of autocracy.

The Tsar's concessions appeared to be a victory for the Constitutional Democrats, who were committed to the political liberalization of Russia. Although the party was composed largely of professionals such as lawyers, university professors, and zemstvo activists, it also gained the support of a small number of industrialists. A majority of its adherents belonged to the privileged class of the nobility.

The aim of the Kadet Party was to rid the country of the autocratic regime and replace it with a liberal democratic form of government. The party favored universal suffrage—adult men and women were to be granted the right to vote, a reform not yet adopted by the leading democracies in the West. To achieve their goals, the Kadets urged the election of a constituent assembly that would write a liberal constitution to replace the autocratic form of government.

The party played a leading role in the First Duma, which met in 1906; in the opposition to the Tsar that emerged during World War I; and in the initial cabinet of the Provisional Government in 1917 after the fall of the monarchy. Pavel Miliukov, a professional historian and journalist, was the party's most prominent leader. He served briefly as Foreign Minister in 1917, but was forced to leave office within weeks of his appointment because of his ardent support of the war and the annexation of Turkish territory.

Somewhat later, the leaders of conservative liberalism who were satisfied with the reforms issued by the Tsar formed the Union of October 17, which favored a monarchy that retained considerable power over legislation. Finally, the ultraconservatives founded the Union of the Russian People (URP) to organize the masses in defense of the old order. The parties of the Left—the Bolsheviks, Mensheviks, and Socialist Revolutionaries—remained active, so that Russia now had a vibrant political party system, one of the major results of the revolution.

Counterrevolution

For several months in late 1905 and early 1906, the government sought to restore a semblance of order and stability, but the obstacles proved insuperable. The demobilization of more than one million soldiers still in the Far East proceeded slowly, because of frequent strikes on the railroads. Frustrated and angry, many soldiers became unruly. To ease political tensions, Witte ordered the release of some political prisoners, but liberals remained dissatisfied and refused to support the Prime Minister. Most troubling, Witte's attempts to establish his government's authority took place against a background of mass violence, one of the more puzzling outbursts of raw passion in 1905. Moreover, precisely at the moment when the autocracy was at its weakest, when it had been compelled to grant its first major concession, the defenders of the old order unleashed their most intense and ferocious attack on the advocates of change. This resort to brute force threatened to undermine the new order before it could be consolidated.

The violence that erupted in the streets and countryside of the empire was as sudden as it was widespread. Although Jews, widely detested for their religious beliefs, were the principal target, they were not the only ones to come under attack. The rampaging mobs also targeted the intelligentsia; anyone, in fact, who was presumed to have participated in the movement to extract the Manifesto of 17 October from the Tsar, or who simply rejoiced in it. All in all, 690 anti-Jewish massacres (known as pogroms) occurred, primarily in the southwestern provinces; 820 people were killed and between 7,000 and 8,000 injured. The damage to property during the pogroms has been valued at 62 million rubles. Although the government in St. Petersburg does not seem to have been a major instigator of the pogroms, local authorities frequently turned a blind eye to the violence and sometimes even participated in it.

In addition to mob violence in the cities, Witte was also confronted with a new wave of disturbances in the countryside and a rash of mutinies in the army and navy. The relative calm in the villages in the late summer and early fall of 1905 ended with large-scale disorders that broke out in Chernigov (northern Ukraine) on 23 October 1905, when about two thousand peasants plundered several landlords' estates. The unrest spread quickly, reaching its climax in November (when there were 796 major and minor incidents), by which time the turbulence in the cities had already receded. It has been estimated that during the last months of 1905, three times as many regions suffered major disturbances as in the spring and early summer; altogether, 428 districts in the forty-seven provinces of European Russia were affected, as well as parts of Caucasia, the Baltic provinces, and Poland. A major reason for the upsurge in violence in the countryside was the conviction by the peasants that they had been kept in the dark by reactionary bureaucrats and landlords about the Tsar's granting of freedom to the people in the October Manifesto. Freedom, as interpreted by the peasants, meant the right to attack landlords' estates.

No less threatening to public order was the extensive disaffection in the army and navy. Many soldiers and sailors also chose to interpret the October Manifesto according to their own lights. They persuaded themselves that the Tsar's concession gave them license to overturn the regulations they found burdensome. Of course, the document made no reference at all to civil liberties for men in uniform, but that was immaterial. The October Manifesto produced a profound change in the psychology of men who had been indoctrinated to accept discipline as the prime virtue. That psychological change opened the dikes to a veritable flood of mutinies.

The first occurred on the Kronstadt naval base on 26–7 October, and by mid-December 1905 a total of 211 had broken out in the army. Some involved a considerable amount of violence and plundering of businesses, but in most cases the men simply refused to obey orders, left their barracks, held meetings to discuss current affairs, and talked back to officers. The navy was so riddled with unrest that the government feared that it could no longer be relied upon to carry out its mission. In late November, a large group of officers (mainly in the Far East and Siberia) gave indications of openly supporting the opposition.

The government was never totally bereft of loyal troops. Even among the infantry, the branch most directly affected by mutinies, two-thirds of the units remained unaffected by serious unrest. Then, on 6 December, the government decided on a series of military reforms—increase in pay and meat rations, abolition of forced labor, and reduction in the term of service—which helped restore calm. By mid-December, the government felt secure enough to order troops to put down the workers and peasants who continued to resist its authority. This step proved instrumental in turning back the tide of revolution.

Days of liberty

The issuance of the October Manifesto ushered in the so-called Days of Liberty, a period of some two months during which ordinary Russians enjoyed a degree of freedom few would have dreamed of a year earlier. Newspapers and journals of all political movements—liberal, Marxist, Socialist Revolutionary, anarchist—were sold freely on the streets of St. Petersburg and elsewhere. In many ways, the most dramatic development was the vast expansion of operations by the soviets. In addition to functioning as strike organizers, they established regular contact with city councils and often secured access to public halls for their meetings; in some regions, local organs of government even honored the soviet's request that they give financial aid to unemployed workers. The pacesetter was the St. Petersburg soviet, which did not hesitate to send directives to government agencies such as the postal service and the railroads; on several occasions, it entered into negotiations with the St. Petersburg City Council—and once even with the Prime Minister himself. It sent numerous inquiries to government offices, and the latter were sufficiently impressed by the soviet's authority to go to the trouble of answering. The soviet also sponsored collections for unemployed workers and distributed thirty kopeks a day to needy adults and ten to fifteen kopeks to children. Moreover, it set up several inexpensive dining halls for the unemployed and their families.

According to Colonel A.V. Gerasimov, the Chief of the St. Petersburg secret police force (*Okhrana*), the boldest undertaking of the soviet in the capital was the establishment of its own militia, whose members, identified by special armbands, 'interfered in the affairs of the police, gave [them] orders and made demands of them.' It was not uncommon, Gerasimov continued, for 'confused [police] officers to give in to the requests of militiamen'. On one occasion, a militiaman demanded that a policeman clean out a pit in a garbage-strewn yard because the odor was unbearable. The policeman meekly obliged. The soviet's power became so far-reaching that the newspaper *Novoe vremia* complained that there were really two governments, one led by Count Witte and one by G. S. Krustalev-Nosar (chairman of the St. Petersburg soviet), and no one knew who would arrest whom first.

The last gasp of the revolution

Flushed with success, the revolutionary Left overplayed its hand and began to press for more concessions. It decided, on its own inititative, to introduce the eight-hour day and supported a new round of industrial strikes, several of which fizzled out, indicating that the tide was turning in favor of the government. However, the Left's enthusiasm for revolution did not flag, and in November some radical activists began to espouse armed conflict. This radicalization also prompted a few revolutionary leaders to advance ideas that went beyond the previous predictions of Marxist theorists. In *Nachalo*, a Menshevik paper that appeared legally in Russia, Leon Trotsky advocated the theory of permanent revolution—first advanced in that paper by his colleague and 'mentor,' Parvus (the adopted name of Alexander Helphand)—which explicitly abandoned the traditional Marxist notion that backward Russia must undergo a more or less prolonged period of bourgeois domination before the socialist revolution could be staged. The Russian proletariat, according to Trotsky, had demonstrated greater energy and determination than its counterpart in Western Europe and would therefore be the pathfinder in the struggle for socialism:

> There is no stage, [he wrote] in the bourgeois revolution at which this force [the Russian proletariat] could become satiated, for it is driven forward by the iron logic of class interest. The law of self-preservation dictates to the proletariat a program of permanent revolution. The proletariat accomplishes the fundamental tasks of democracy and then, at a certain moment, the logic of its struggle to consolidate its power confronts it with problems that are purely socialist. Revolutionary permanency is established between our minimum and maximum programs.

The Moscow Committee of Social Democrats agreed with this analysis, and in October 1905 it adopted a resolution calling for the 'immediate preparation for a new decisive battle.' The Socialist Revolutionaries, who had been the first to expound the 'theory

of permanent revolution,' and had favored an armed assault on
the autocracy since the beginning of 1905, welcomed the new
strategy. Reports that reached St. Petersburg in November and
December from such outlying regions of the empire as Chita
in southeastern Siberia, Novorossiisk, Irkutsk, Krasnoiarsk, and
the Baltic provinces, indicating that soviets or other oppositional
groups were assuming the authority of local organs of government, further emboldened the militants.

Witte responded to the growing tension between the government and the opposition with a move that recalled the worst days
of tsarist arbitrariness. On 26 November, infantrymen and Cossacks
surrounded the headquarters of the Free Economic Society and
arrested the president of the soviet, Khrustalev-Nosar, together
with several deputies. The soviet immediately elected a new presidium of three men, among them Trotsky. The presidium wasted no
time in launching a counterattack. On 27 November, it passed a
resolution calling on its followers to prepare for an uprising.

Unexpectedly, Moscow now became the main focus of the
conflict between the government and the opposition. Much
more so in Moscow than in St. Petersburg, the labor movement
received its 'organizational guidance' from the white-collar workers in the nonmanufacturing sector of the economy. These workers were more extensively exposed to radical ideas and therefore
more easily captivated by the slogans of extremists. According to
the German consul in Moscow, immediately after the general
strike of October ended in Moscow it was clear that:

> ... beneath the apparent calm ... there is concealed a
> feverish movement that is gradually affecting ever more
> strata of the population ... Every week, new publications
> appear that openly preach violent revolution, and every
> day one can read about the emergence of new groups of
> employees or workers, who for the most part immediately
> join socialist organizations.

A new wave of work stoppages erupted and increasingly strikers made threats or used force against their employers as well as against workers who crossed the picket lines.

In light of the growing militancy of both the government and the opposition, the question, often raised by historians, of who provoked the violence seems pointless. As V. M. Zenzinov, a prominent Socialist Revolutionary, put it many years later: 'The revolution and the government were like two persons who had already taken aim at each other with pistols. The only question was, who would be the first to pull the trigger.'

On 6 December, the Moscow Soviet, attended by about 120 deputies, issued an official appeal to all workers to begin a 'general political strike' at noon the following day. The appeal stated categorically that the aim was to 'finally overthrow the criminal tsarist government' and to 'proclaim a democratic republic.' For a few days, it looked as though the revolutionaries might prevail, but then Admiral F.V. Dubasov, the recently appointed Governor-General of Moscow, after some hesitant moves, unleashed his forces, which used light artillery—never before applied against Russian subjects—to subdue the strikers. This action infuriated even people unsympathetic to the radicals. For eight days bloody battles raged in the city, but the civilians could not withstand the onslaughts of the army. When it was over, 1,059 Muscovites, most of whom were civilians not involved in the fighting, had been killed. Of these, 137 were women and 86 were children. Twenty-five policemen and nine soldiers lost their lives. This was only the beginning of the carnage in Moscow, for the authorities unleashed a crackdown. There followed numerous executions—without any judicial proceedings—of workers and students, on the mere suspicion of their having taken part in the rising. In addition, hundreds were arrested, and many were savagely beaten. Even people who had opposed the excesses of the revolutionaries were appalled.

Suppression of the revolution

The impact of the Moscow uprising on the course of the revolution can hardly be exaggerated. Since he had assumed the office of Prime Minister, Witte had insisted that order would have to be restored before he could proceed with reform, but for two and a half months he had been relatively restrained in seeking to rein in the militant opposition. On 15 December, however, he decided that a new approach was needed. Whenever the army was called in to pacify an unruly crowd, it must deal 'decisively and mercilessly' with 'all who resist with weapons in their hands.' He told General V. U. Sollogub in Riga that the radicals in his region were so bloodthirsty that 'there is no way to suppress the revolution except by ruthless means.'

The government now resorted to its most devastating and brutal weapon, the punitive expedition, organized attacks by small groups of specially selected troops in regions either controlled by radicals or in a state of chaos. The goal was to root out disorder and to intimidate the population. It amounted to a form of state terror directed at Russia's own subjects. At least ten punitive expeditionary forces, ranging widely in size and firepower, were dispatched to various parts of the empire: the Baltic provinces, Siberia, the Ukraine, and the Caucasus. The authorities also placed a vastly increased number of regions under exceptional laws. By the spring of 1906, about 69 percent of the provinces and regions of the Russian Empire were either completely or partially subject to various emergency codes. Moreover, on 6 December the Tsar signed a *ukase* that granted governors and commanders in any region not under exceptional laws the right to issue permits to wealthy landowners to form militias with their own funds. These semi-independent armed forces sprang up in the countryside early in 1906 and played a significant role in the campaign against agrarian unrest.

The government's repressive policies proved highly effective. Within about four months, the revolutionary movement was in retreat everywhere, incapable of holding the line against the authorities. Public opinion was shocked by the cold-blooded repression, all the more so as it became clear that many victories won by the opposition in October 1905 would be rescinded, marking the defeat of the revolution. In fact, the situation was rather more complicated. True, the government still controlled the levers of power and had regained much of its self-confidence and authority, but the conflict that had erupted early in 1905 was not yet fully resolved. The opposition remained vibrant enough to continue the struggle, and could take advantage of certain concessions it had secured in October 1905. The revolution now entered a new phase in which politics was the most characteristic, though by no means the only, mode of struggle.

Early in December 1905, the government enacted a law in keeping with its promise during the general strike that vastly increased the number of eligible voters who could participate in the elections to the Duma. Somewhere between twenty and twenty-five million male citizens over the age of twenty-four were permitted to cast ballots. Eligibility was not democratic as we understand the word: in a complex system the population was divided into four *curiae*—landowners, peasants, town dwellers, and workers—and the landowners and peasants were assigned a preponderance of electors, who made the final selection of representatives. Convinced that the peasants would vote for conservatives, the government thought it had cleverly manipulated the arrangements to provide it with a majority. In April 1906, when the results of the election were tabulated, it turned out that the Duma was overwhelmingly hostile to the old order. Of the 478 representatives who were seated at the first session, only 13 belonged to the moderate Octobrist Party (strong supporters of the October Manifesto) and not a single one had been elected by the extreme Right, which still favored autocracy. The Kadets and their adherents captured 185 seats and dominated the proceedings. That alignment set the stage for the fierce political conflicts that prevailed during the final fifteen months or so of the revolution.

The Tsar reasserts his authority

Tsar Nicholas, it now became evident, had no intention of surrendering his power. Consequently, parliament and the government clashed with one another for well over a year. It did not help that before the First Duma met, the clever Witte was replaced as Prime Minister by the colorless, weak, and lazy I. L. Goremykin, who had no strong urge to exercise leadership and for whom compromise was simply not part of his lexicon. The feuds touched on the critical issues that had divided Russia since the beginning of the revolutionary upheaval: the transformation of the country's political system into a liberal constitutional monarchy and agrarian reform that included the compulsory alienation of private land. The Duma had been in session for only forty-two days when the Tsar used his authority to dissolve it (in July 1906). The government permitted new elections, which it expected would yield a more compliant legislature, but the voters opted for a Duma well to the left of the first one.

Nevertheless, the Octobrists increased their strength from 13 to 44, and the extremists on the Right, who lacked representation in the First Duma, succeeded in electing ten deputies and could count on the support of some 54 from other factions. The number of left-wing deputies jumped from 111 to 222, with the Social Democrats, Socialist Revolutionaries, and Popular Socialists together amassing 118 seats (as against 17 in the First Duma), and the other party of the Left (the Trudoviks), 104. The center parties suffered a major decline: 99 seats were won by the Kadets and their adherents; in the First Duma these groups could count on the support of 185 deputies. The Muslim group elected 30 and the Cossack group 17. The Polish Kolo raised its number of deputies from 32 to 46. The representation of nonpartisans decreased the most, from 112 to 50.

The Cossacks

The Cossacks—in old Slavonic the word means 'free men'—constituted one of the more colorful social groups in the Russian Empire. First mentioned in written records in the mid-fifteenth century, they lived in various areas of the country, known as 'host regions', and enjoyed a considerable degree of self-government. The males, famous horsemen, were outstanding professional warriors and also reputed to be fierce pirates and conquerors of territory near their host regions. Although they numbered only four and a half million early in the twentieth century, three hundred thousand Cossacks fought in the Russian army in World War I.

The Cossacks had a history of rebellion against the government. In the seventeenth and eighteenth centuries their leaders—Stenka Razin and Emelian Pugachev, respectively—fought bitterly against government forces in support of peasant rights. In both cases, the Cossacks were defeated, but they managed to retain their separate status. By the nineteenth and early twentieth centuries, the Cossacks had switched sides and often played a significant role in suppressing unrest directed at the tsarist autocracy. Frequently, they assumed a major role in pogroms—violent attacks—against Jews. However, during the unrest in March 1917, which led to the downfall of the tsarist autocracy, they refused to come to the aid of the besieged Tsar. By 1918, many had gone over to the side of the opposition to the Bolsheviks. The Cossacks lost their privileges under Communism and during World War II their loyalty was divided; some fought for the Soviet Union and others joined the German army after it invaded Russia. Although the Cossacks no longer enjoy a separate status, a fair number still take pride in their roots.

In the meantime, P. A. Stolypin, formerly Governor of Grodno, and then Minister of Internal Affairs for several months in 1906, had taken over as Prime Minister. Intelligent, and more flexible than his predecessor, he succeeded in introducing reform in the agricultural sector that made it easier for peasants to acquire land. This was his most significant achievement, and had the outbreak of war in 1914 not put a halt to its implementation, it might have enabled Russia to avoid the Bolshevik revolution, although the autocracy would probably have been replaced with some form of parliamentary regime.

Stolypin favored other reforms, such as the lifting of some of the restrictions on Jews, but he did not press them if he encountered resistance from the Tsar. He believed in monarchical rule and avoided any action that might seriously weaken Nicholas. He was committed to harsh measures to root out lawlessness and terror, which continued to plague the country. It did not take long for Stolypin to run into conflict with the Duma. Tensions reached a high point when a committee of the legislature adopted a measure favoring expropriation of large amounts of privately owned land for distribution to peasants. In one of his more dramatic speeches, Stolypin appealed to the deputies not to pass the bill: 'The opponents of the State system would like to choose the path of radicalism, a path alien to Russia's historical past, alien to its cultural traditions. They need great upheavals, we need a great Russia.'

Relations between Stolypin and the Duma deteriorated further when the government claimed to have discovered a connection between I. P. Ozol, a Menshevik deputy from Riga, and a military-revolutionary committee that, according to Stolypin, planned 'to provoke an uprising within the army.' The police's evidence in support of this charge was sketchy at best, but that was beside the point. It is now known that the government had decided to stage what can only be characterized as a *coup d'état*. On 3 June 1907, Okhrana (political police) agents entered the Tauride Palace, the meeting place of the Duma, and posted a manifesto of dissolution on the doors. In the manifesto, Tsar Nicholas noted that he was taking the action 'to Our regret' because the legislature had failed to discharge its obligations. Instead of working to promote the well-being of Russia, it had made clear its 'intention to increase unrest and to promote the disintegration of the state.' He also announced that a new Duma would be elected and would meet six months later, on 1 November.

The government made sure that the new legislature would be strikingly different from the first two. It issued a law that reduced the size of the Duma from 542 to 442, almost entirely at the expense of the outlying regions of the empire. The steppe and Turkestan regions, the vast Turgai, Ural, and Iakutsk oblasts, the nomadic peoples of Astrakhan and Stavropol, and the Siberian Cossacks, lost their representation completely. The delegations of the Poles, Armenians, and Tatars were sharply reduced. As a consequence, the Poles, with a population of about eleven million, would elect fourteen deputies, two of whom had to be Russian; in the Second Duma, the Polish delegation had numbered forty-six. The roughly six million people of Transcaucasia would elect seven deputies, one of whom would have to be ethnically Russian. By contrast, the province of Kursk, with a mostly Russian population of two and a half million, was assigned eleven deputies; and Tambov, with an overwhelmingly Russian population of three million, would elect twelve. In addition, the law favored the affluent over the masses: the peasants would choose only half as many electors (those who made the final selections of deputies) as in 1906, and the landowners a third more than in the previous election.

In the fifty-one provinces of European Russia, landowners would gain roughly 49.6 percent of the electors, city dwellers 26.2 percent, the peasants 22.7 percent, and industrial workers 2.3 percent. In slightly more than half of these provinces, landowners by themselves selected a majority of the electors, and in the remaining provinces they could obtain a majority by forming alliances with one or another urban group. To reduce the election of urban liberals, eighteen of twenty cities were deprived of the right to choose their own deputies, by being merged with provincial constituencies. Women, men under the age of twenty-five, students, and soldiers and sailors in active service were not franchised. Although the voting was fairly straightforward and direct in the large cities, elsewhere the system of indirect balloting was so complicated that the process resembled walking through a labyrinth. The elections were to proceed in three different stages, and the electors who survived the process would meet in the provincial capitals to choose the deputies. As a Russian citizen interviewed by the British journalist Harold Williams put it: 'The system is so calculated that, in the end, the big landowners are almost certain to secure a majority, and the peasants returned are usually those who seem to the landowners fairly safe.'

He was right. In the new legislature, Stolypin could generally count on the support of about 300 deputies out of a total of 441. Thus, the dissolution of the Duma and the promulgation of the new electoral law can be said to have marked the final defeat of the revolution. That does not mean that the Revolution of 1905, which might be more accurately designated as the Revolution of 1904–7, left no lasting traces in the country. In later years, Lenin often referred to the first upheaval as the 'dress rehearsal' for 1917, by which he meant that without it 'the victory of the October Revolution in 1917 would have been impossible.' Lenin's description of 1905 was also meant to suggest the inevitability of 1917, since a dress rehearsal is always followed by the first performance. Soviet historians invariably quoted Lenin's pithy comment on 1905, which, they believed, settled the question of why the revolution was a pivotal event in modern history. Although the characterization of the Revolution of 1905 as the dress rehearsal for 1917 is debatable, in some respects the link between the two is indisputable. Bolshevism emerged as a distinct political movement during the first revolution. Strictly speaking, the movement originated in 1902–3, but only after the spread of unrest in 1904 did Lenin and his followers begin to adopt the strategies and tactics that became the key features of Bolshevism, distinguishing it fully from other strands of Marxism. It was also during the ferment of 1905 that the soviet, which played a central role in 1917 and for many years thereafter, was founded.

Equally important, the empire's political system had been changed in important ways in the years from 1904 to 1907. True, the Tsar still claimed to rule as an autocrat, but so long as the Duma continued to function, as it did till the end of the old regime, the claim was not convincing. Neither he nor the bureaucracy could operate as arbitrarily as before. On many vital questions the Tsar and his officials needed the support of the legislature. Although the electoral law of 3 June 1907 deprived the masses of much of their representation, the Duma did not become a mere rubber stamp for the government. That the Duma was a vibrant institution was demonstrated with special force during the crisis of the old regime in 1916 and 1917. A significant majority of the deputies fiercely criticized the autocracy and spoke for large sectors of the nation. The Provisional Government that took control after the Tsar's abdication in March 1917 was the Duma's creation. Without the reforms introduced during the Revolution of 1905, such developments would have been inconceivable.

The multiparty system after 1907 was another legacy of the revolution. Frequent repression of the Left continued, and the Kadets were never recognized as a legal party, but the Kadets, the Social Democrats, and the Popular Socialists, among other parties, were represented in the Dumas, and both liberal and radical deputies often spoke out against official abuses. Despite the restrictions imposed by the government, newspapers and journals could deal with sensitive political and social issues in a way that had been unimaginable before the revolution.

The trade union movement suffered some heavy blows at Stolypin's hands, and from 1907 to 1912 the number of organized workers declined sharply. Nevertheless, workers continued to nurture other 'legal opportunities for collective association, such as clubs, cultural societies, consumer cooperatives, and production cartels.' Those who participated in these organizations constituted a relatively small group, but their experiences stood them in good stead when new opportunities for mass action opened up.

3
The collapse of tsarism

For about a decade after the dissolution of the Second Duma, the Russian leadership did not face a mass movement bent on overturning the tsarist regime, but the political waters were not entirely calm. Unrest in the countryside surfaced periodically, and strikes by workers in various industrial regions were not uncommon. The most dramatic broke out in 1912 in the Lena Goldfields in Siberia, which the army crushed with terrifying brutality, killing some two hundred workers. Far from ending worker unrest, this cruelty spurred workers in other parts of the country to stage strikes during which they voiced economic as well as political demands. In July 1914, a strike movement that often involved violence engulfed various regions. At no time until 1917 did the authorities face the kind of danger to the stability of the state that they had confronted in 1905.

World War I

Once again, the decisive factor in turning deep discontent into revolutionary action was a military conflict that exposed Russia's weakness and recklessness, and caused untold suffering to millions of ordinary citizens. One of the curious aspects of World War I is that no responsible leader wanted to lead his country into battle; if in 1914 the monarchs and ministers had had any inkling of the consequences of the war, they probably would not have given their armies the order to march. When the fighting ended four years later, millions of people had perished, three monarchs had lost their thrones, national boundaries had been changed, often arbitrarily, revolutions had erupted in several countries, and the ensuing bitterness throughout Europe had set the stage for yet another world war even more costly in every respect than the first one.

Ideology, as much as anything else, dictated the policy of Russian statesmen and of Tsar Nicholas II during the international crisis that erupted on 15 June (commonly noted as 28 June in the Gregorian calendar) 1914. On that day, the Archduke Franz Ferdinand, heir to the Habsburg throne, was assassinated, together with his wife, in Sarajevo, the capital of Bosnia, a province populated by Slavs that Austria-Hungary had annexed in 1908. The government in Vienna concluded that the assassination was part of a plan by Serbia to gain control over Bosnia and to establish a new state, Yugoslavia, which was to embrace all southern Slavs. The Austro-Hungarian statesmen feared such a development, because it would most likely lead to the unraveling of their multinational state. They therefore decided on a provocative and aggressive step. They sent an ultimatum to Serbia demanding not only the suppression of all anti-Austrian agitation but also the participation of Austrians in the crackdown. No sovereign government could accept such conditions, and Serbia was no exception. On 15 July (commonly noted as 28 July in the Gregorian calendar), Austria-Hungary declared war on Serbia.

Russia's elite contended that their country, long the protector of 'her little Slav brother,' could not stand aside and allow fellow Slavs to be subjugated. At this early stage of the crisis, Tsar Nicholas, who insisted on playing a key role in foreign affairs, made a decision that demonstrated his failings as a head of state and proved fatal for his country. He ordered the military leaders to mobilize Russia's armed forces, but in response to an urgent plea by Kaiser Wilhelm II of Germany to avoid an irrevocable and provocative action, he rescinded the order and instead called for a partial mobilization, which was to be directed only at Austria-Hungary. When his generals and the foreign minister, S. D. Sazonov, advised him that since the high command had never formulated plans for a partial mobilization, he should revert to the original order; the Tsar complied, setting off a chain reaction that plunged Europe into war. Germany, which was allied with Austria-Hungary, quickly followed suit in mobilizing its own forces, as did France, which was allied with Russia and feared Germany. Great Britain entered the conflict on 22 July (commonly noted as 4 August in the Gregorian calendar) on the side of France, mainly because it, too, feared German domination of the continent. A serious incident in one remote corner of Europe had triggered a world war that no one in a position of authority had expected or wanted.

Initially, the onset of war was greeted by a wave of patriotism throughout Russia, but as in most military conflicts the enthusiasm did not last long. In the Russia of 1914 there were more than the usual reasons for the public's quick change of heart. For one thing, it soon became evident that the authorities were not in a position to wage war effectively. The Tsar appointed his uncle, Grand Duke Nicholas Nikolaevich, as Commander in Chief, granting him enormous power and declaring him responsible to the ruler alone. The Grand Duke was totally unsuited for the post, as he himself admitted when he told associates that he did not know what to do. His only attributes were his extraordinary good looks and popularity among the troops. A year after the beginning of hostilities, Nicholas relieved the Grand Duke and made an even worse choice: he assumed the position himself. The Tsar knew even less about warfare than his uncle, but that was not the only reason his assumption of supreme military command was an egregious mistake. From now on, he could not blame others for blunders and defeats on the battlefield. The autocrat became the focus of the growing public discontent with all aspects of the war effort.

The army was ill-prepared for war. Most senior officers were mediocrities who had advanced to high positions only because seniority, not ability, was the determining factor in promotions. The War Ministry focused on building up as large an army as possible: by September 1915, it had mobilized 9.7 million men; two years later that figure had jumped to 15 million, probably the largest army in history. However, in war, as in most human endeavors, quantity does not make up for poor quality. Many of the rank and file were illiterate and unaware of what the war was all about. There were not enough training facilities, and draftees were often demoralized by remaining idle for months. A shortage of junior and non-commissioned officers further delayed the training of recruits. Finally, and perhaps most harmful to morale, the army had to contend with scarcities of equipment of every kind, including food. Equipment lost during battles could not easily be replaced because of the small size and inefficiency of the country's industrial base. During an offensive, it was not uncommon for the second and subsequent rows of infantrymen to lack weapons; they had to wait until some of their comrades had fallen so that they could pick up their weapons and continue the advance.

Initially, the Russian army scored some victories. In August 1914, it advanced into eastern Prussia in an attempt to relieve the French, who were being attacked at their borders and might have lost Paris had it not been for the offensive of the tsarist army. Later that month, when Marshal Paul von Hindenburg launched a counterattack in the Battle of Tannenberg, the Russians were routed, losing some 300,000 men and 650 guns. Even more serious was the psychological impact of the defeat; Russian soldiers became convinced that the well-trained, highly disciplined, and well-led German army could never be defeated. The Russian advance into Galicia (now Poland) was more successful, but only because the Austro-Hungarian army was similarly ineffective, in part because its ranks contained many Slavs, Ukrainians, and Czechs, who felt little loyalty to their country. When the Germans launched a counter-offensive in May 1915, the tide turned quickly. The Russians were forced to give up virtually all the gains they had made nine months earlier.

By this time, enthusiasm for the war had started to decline sharply. At first, the only reason the government could give for waging war was the brotherly love of Russians for the Slavs, but most Russians could muster little affection for their distant brothers, the Serbs. Then the people were motivated to fight the Germans because they had invaded Russia. Turkey, which had joined the conflict on the side of Germany, had long been despised by many Russians. In mid-1915, the government came up with another reason to fight on with enthusiasm. It reached an agreement with Great Britain and France that after the war, Russia would be given control over Constantinople and the adjoining straits that marked the boundary between Europe and Asia, long a dream of Russian expansionists. A year later, the two allies, eager to prop up the government, promised Russia several districts in Asiatic Turkey. A goodly number within educated and liberal circles reacted positively to the promises, which were kept secret until 1917, but the vast majority of the people had never heard of those territories and could not be persuaded to risk their well-being or their lives for them.

As the war dragged on, domestic conditions worsened at an alarming pace. By 1917, 37 percent of the male population of working age had been drafted, creating a severe shortage of labor. Often, inexperienced people were hired as replacements, and productivity declined. At the same time, since owners of large estates, which were the primary producers of food for the market, could not find enough workers, shortages became an increasingly worrisome problem. With the retreat of the Russian army, large fertile areas were lost, further decreasing the food supply. Even so, the government might have found enough food for the army had the railroad system not broken down. One reason for the breakdown was that most of the lines in the western regions had fallen under the control of the enemy; another was poor management of the railways still available to the Russian authorities. Moreover, by 1917 the number of locomotives had declined from twenty thousand to nine thousand, so that it became ever more difficult to transport goods. In 1916, the government introduced food rationing, but implementation of this measure turned out to be chaotic and inefficient. It was widely disregarded by shopkeepers, who raised prices at a pace that left many people unable to buy the most essential products.

The defeats on the battlefield and the economic hardships at home increased political tensions between various sectors of society. On the one hand, Nicholas insisted that to win the war he had to govern more dictatorially than ever before. On the other hand, the Duma and local institutions such as the zemstvos, and some non-governmental bodies, increased their sphere of activities in the hope of finding ways to cope with the numerous problems facing the country.

The nefarious influence of Rasputin

The autocrat took his role as Commander in Chief seriously and in August 1915 he moved to Mogilev, where the military headquarters were located. He received daily reports on the military situation, but left the conduct of the war to General M.V. Alekseev, who was the actual Commander in Chief. The Tsar's presence in Mogilev did not lift the spirits of the troops or the people, and did not lead to victories against the German army. On the contrary, disgruntlement with the authorities increased as news spread of the growing influence at the tsarist court of Grigori Efimovich Rasputin, an unkempt and semi-literate monk whose rise to prominence in the late imperial period is one of the more bizarre indications of the degenerate state of Russian politics.

Not much is known about Rasputin's early life. He was born in 1872 in the province of Tobolsk, 250 miles east of the Ural Mountains; as a young man, he acquired a reputation for horse-stealing and lust. In the early 1890s, he was married and sired three children, but neither marriage nor fatherhood restrained his search for sexual adventures. His wife did not mind. 'He has enough for all,' she explained. At some point, Rasputin under-went a religious experience of sorts. He joined an illegal mystical sect and disappeared from Siberia. For a few years, he adopted the lifestyle of the *stranniki* (holy wanderers), ascetics who traveled throughout the country and lived on charity. After two pilgrim-ages to Jerusalem, Rasputin showed up at the religious academy in St. Petersburg in December 1903. The monk Illiodor, who met him at the time, remembered him as a 'stocky peasant of middle height, with ragged and dirty hair falling over his shoul-ders, tangled beard, and steely-grey eyes, deep set under the bushy eyebrows, which sometimes almost sank into pin points, and a strong body odor.' Illiodor and other clergymen, impressed by Rasputin's declaration that he wished to repent for his sins by serving God, helped him get settled in St. Petersburg.

Somehow, Rasputin persuaded dignitaries in the capital that he could perform miracles. He first demonstrated his skills by allegedly curing a sick dog beloved by Grand Duke Nicholas Nikolaevich. Late in 1905, Rasputin was introduced to the Tsar and Tsarina, and immediately captivated the royal couple by stop-ping the bleeding of their only son, Alexis, who suffered from hemophilia. Apparently, Rasputin achieved the feat by means of hypnosis; there is evidence that such a procedure can work. In any case, the Tsarina concluded that Rasputin 'was a holy man, almost a Christ.' She also interpreted his appearance at the court as a sign of the mystical union between the peasants and the autocracy; a man of the people, she reasoned, had come to save the dynasty.

Rasputin conducted innumerable affairs, often with ladies close to the imperial court who were convinced that God revealed himself in his words and that his 'kisses and embraces sanctified each of his faithful disciples.' Some men actually felt honored to be cuckolded by the lascivious monk. However, many people in St. Petersburg society, including respected political leaders, were scandalized and publicly denounced Rasputin as a 'fornicator of human souls and bodies.' None of the expressions of outrage bothered the Tsarina. In fact, during the Tsar's long absences at the front she relied more than ever on the 'holy monk's' advice as she played a growing role in shaping domestic policies. Early in 1916, for example, the Tsarina urged Nicholas to appoint the incompetent Boris Stürmer as Prime Minister because he greatly valued Rasputin and 'completely believes in [his] wonderful, God-sent wisdom.' Unfortunately for Russia— and for the autocracy—Nicholas heeded her advice.

Even archconservatives who revered the autocracy and scorned liberalism and democracy could not bear the embarrassment of this state of affairs. Convinced that Rasputin was undermining the monarchy as well as the state, in December 1916 several took it upon themselves to assassinate the monk. Prince Felix Yusupov, who was married to one of the Tsar's nieces, organized a conspiracy; he invited the 'Holy Devil' to his home for a party. The host plied Rasputin with poisoned wine and cakes, which the monk devoured with few ill effects. Yusupov then fired several shots into the monk, and with the help of the other conspirators, dumped him in the Neva River. They had hoped that the murder of Rasputin would impel conservatives to join a movement to save the monarchy. It was too late. The people of Russia were thoroughly disillusioned with the war and refused to tolerate the hardships it had caused any longer. Only the Tsar and Tsarina and their most loyal followers continued to believe that Russia was pursuing a path that would lead to victory.

The government flounders

The signs of political disarray were visible at all levels of government. Ministers who had been appointed on the recommendation of the Tsarina and Rasputin often remained in office for short periods, only to be followed by even more incompetent successors. A. D. Protopopov, the Minister of the Interior, was allowed to stay in office for several months in late 1916, even though it had become clear that he no longer was fully in command of his faculties. To describe the many changes in 1915–16 in the cabinet, the ultra-conservative Duma deputy V. M. Purishkevich coined the term 'ministerial leapfrog,' which brought ridicule on the Tsar's conduct of affairs. A fair number of people had even persuaded themselves that Rasputin and a group of pro-Germans at the tsarist court were trying to undermine the war effort. This was not true but that did not change any minds.

Although the Duma surrendered much of its power shortly after the onset of the war, it did not disappear completely from the political arena. After voting for war credits in July 1914 it adjourned, which meant that the government could rule by decree. The deputies continued to meet informally, and they played an active role in organizing relief efforts for people enduring wartime deprivations. At first, most deputies enthusiastically supported Russia's war effort, but within a year they began to suspect that the authorities were bungling affairs at home and on the battlefield. At one of their informal meetings, they issued a series of requests to the Tsar and the government: to convoke the Duma so that it could participate in running the government, to dismiss the most disreputable ministers, to give non-bureaucratic agencies more leeway in running affairs, and, finally, to form a new government that could count on the confidence and support of the nation. Implementation of these measures would not have required a formal change in the Constitution, which still accorded vast powers to the monarchy, but the Tsar granted only minor concessions, such as the dismissal of a few of the most despised ministers.

The concessions did not satisfy the deputies, who were appalled at the poor showing of the army, the incompetence of the military high command, and the insensitive handling of the refugees who had fled the advancing German army, as well as the failure to put a stop to the spate of anti-Semitic pogroms. In despair, in July 1915 the deputies formed a Progressive Bloc that included members of six of the leading parties in the legislature, and even a few representatives from moderate conservative parties. The bloc called for a government that would enjoy the confidence of the country and honor the rule of law. A majority of the ministers wanted to discuss the demands with the deputies, but the prime minister at the time, Goremykin, who had led the government some years earlier without distinction, denounced the bloc as unconstitutional and prorogued the Duma. This ill-conceived move exacerbated political tensions, which reached a high point on 1 November 1916, when P. N. Miliukov, the leader of the Kadets, publicly raised questions about the loyalty to Russia of the authorities in St. Petersburg. In what the historian Melissa Kirschke Stockdale has described as 'the most notorious address in the history of the Duma,' Miliukov cited numerous examples of treachery by senior officials. The most dramatic case involved Goremykin's successor, Prime Minister Stürmer, whose private secretary, Ivan Manasevich-Manuilov, was accused of being in the pay of the German government. The evidence against the suspect appeared in a German newspaper and he was arrested, but the police released him without putting him on trial, apparently because he had succeeded in handing over some of the money he had received from the Germans to none other than the Prime Minister himself.

Miliukov ended his speech with a recital of Stürmer's worst decisions and after each one he posed a provocative question: 'Is this stupidity or is it treason?' To each question the deputies who filled the hall shouted three different responses: 'Stupidity!' 'Treason!' 'Both!' The government immediately ordered the press not to publish any reports on the speech, but it was a futile gesture. Word of the speech reached the public when enterprising citizens managed to produce and distribute many thousands of copies. Miliukov was transformed into a national celebrity.

By this time, discontent with the government's handling of every aspect of the war and the economy was rampant throughout the country. Its clearest manifestation was the increase in industrial strikes. At the beginning of the war, labor had refrained from ordering work stoppages and not until the spring of 1915 was this policy abandoned. Throughout 1915, over one thousand strikes broke out, involving 550,000 workers. That number rose somewhat in 1916 and the unrest became even more extensive during the first two months of 1917. On the anniversary of Bloody Sunday, close to 140,000 workers, from almost half the factories in the capital, left their jobs. In mid-February, some 84,000 walked out, bringing fifty-two factories to a halt. On the whole, during the war the strikers focused much more on economic than domestic political demands and at times the people who left their jobs voiced hostility toward the foreign enemy, Germany. Whatever the motive, the increasing willingness of workers to engage in illegal strikes was an ominous sign.

The last Tsar

It is difficult to predict the outbreak of a revolution. Hardships may be intense and many people may find themselves in dire straits, but the decision to defy state authority brings enormous risks and is rarely planned. Revolutions generally break out after an unexpected incident arouses mass anger. Certainly, in the early days of 1917, no one predicted the kind of upheaval that soon enveloped the Russian Empire. Even Lenin, probably the most dedicated student and the most fervent advocate of revolution of his time, could not read the writing on the wall. P. B. Axelrod, a leading Menshevik, said of him that: '… there is not another man who for twenty-four hours of the day is taken up with the revolution, who has no other thoughts but thoughts of revolution, and who, even in his sleep, dreams of nothing but revolution. Just try and handle such a fellow.' Nevertheless, in a lecture to young workers in Zurich in January 1917, Lenin predicted that only his listeners would have the good fortune to witness the '… victory of socialism. We of the older generation may not live to see the decisive battles of this coming revolution.'

Lenin cannot be faulted for failing to foresee the evolution of events in Russia. The upheaval that began in Petrograd late in February 1917 and led to two revolutions—the first for democracy and the second for socialism—was unexpected, leaderless, and spontaneous. Many historians and participants in the revolutionary events (on both the Right and the Left) reject an explanation that stresses spontaneity: it makes the historical process too prosaic and lacking in purposefulness. Thus, Leon Trotsky, who became the second most important leader of Bolshevism and wrote a stirring history of 1917, contended that although no Bolshevik leaders of the first rank were in Petrograd in early 1917, the workers who staged the demonstrations had been schooled in the ideology of Bolshevism and had gained revolutionary experience in 1905 under the guidance of Lenin's party. As a consequence, the workers in the streets of Petrograd were class-conscious activists driven by firmly held convictions. On the other hand, George Katkov, a learned historian and devotee of the monarchical principle and the Romanov dynasty, contended that the blame for the autocracy's collapse must be placed on the liberals, and even more so, on the machinations of the German government. The liberals' relentless campaign and numerous intrigues against the government during the wartime years had undermined public confidence in the authorities. At the same time, the German government, according to Katkov, in an effort to subvert Russia's war effort, had given substantial sums of money to Russian revolutionaries in 1916 to enable them to mobilize the masses for demonstrations against the regime; those demonstrations evolved into the revolutionary upheaval of 1917.

Leon Trotsky

Among Russian revolutionary leaders, no one had a more variegated and troubled life than Leon Trotsky. Born into a secular and well-to-do family in 1879, in a small town in the Ukraine, he changed his name from Bronshtein to Trotsky in 1902. He had been active in revolutionary causes since the age of seventeen, and in 1898 he joined the Russian Marxist movement, then known as the Russian Social Democratic Labor Party, and quickly became an influential member.

As a theorist and organizer, Trotsky was Lenin's equal, and as a writer and orator, he was his superior. Trotsky was unmatched as a phrasemaker, and when he confronted difficult situations he knew how to extricate himself with a clever turn of phrase. However, he lacked one quality that Lenin possessed in abundance: steadfastness. Lenin founded the Bolshevik movement in 1903 and never strayed from its core principles. On the other hand, Trotsky initially supported the Mensheviks. Then, from 1904 to 1917, he identified himself as a 'non-factional social democrat' and, returning to Russia in May 1917, founded a faction that was neither Menshevik nor Bolshevik. He soon joined the Leninists, however, and remained a firm supporter of Bolshevism as he interpreted it for the rest of his life.

Lenin had one other gift that Trotsky lacked: the ability to judge character. Lenin realized that Stalin could not be trusted to be a judicious leader, which he made clear in the testament he wrote shortly before his death. By contrast, Trotsky could not imagine that a person so lacking in intellectual depth and originality as Stalin could rise to leadership of a party that placed a premium on the mastery of abstruse ideas. This failure to understand the workings of politics cost Trotsky dearly—not only his position in the Communist movement, but eventually, his life.

In fact, the strikes that broke out in January and February in Petrograd were inspired primarily by economic motives. Petrograd was suffering from a serious shortage of bread, a staple for the vast majority of Russians. Even though the city apparently had enough flour to last several more days, the inadequate supply of fuel made it impossible for many bakeries to operate. Many workers went into the streets to protest these conditions, and on 22 February the management of the huge Putilov Works locked out their workers, who then joined the marchers and appealed to other workers to follow their example. 23 February was International Women's Day, and after listening to speeches on the plight of the masses, numerous women employed in industry, as well as many who had spent hours in bread queues, poured into the streets. The demonstrators demanded bread and, as the historian William Henry Chamberlin put it, 'here and there red flags appeared with inscriptions: "Down with Autocracy".' The police dispersed the crowd with little difficulty and without using force.

A day later, on 24 February, strikers again appeared on the streets; the number had increased to at least 200,000. The Cossacks refused to charge the crowds, but none of the senior officials seemed to be particularly concerned; they assumed that this was just another demonstration of public discontent that would quickly fade. On 26 February, however, protesters surged onto the streets of the capital once more, and by now they had become larger than ever, about 400,000, according to reliable estimates. Several policemen and soldiers fired into the crowds and dispersed them. As before, it was widely believed that the government had beaten back the opposition and that calm would return to Petrograd.

Yet during the night of 26 February a dramatic decision by soldiers in the barracks entirely changed the course of events. The men of the Pavlovskii Regiment announced that they would no longer fire at the protesters. The soldiers' grievances differed from those of the civilians who had taken to the streets, but they were no less afflictive. Some 160,000 soldiers in the Petrograd area lived in barracks built to accommodate 20,000. In addition, officers treated the enlisted men as inferiors; as well as being addressed by the familiar 'thou,' the men were not allowed to travel in public streetcars. A fair number of the conscripts were not young; already in their thirties and forties, they claimed they had been drafted illegally. When the Pavlovskii Regiment was ordered to march into the streets on 27 February, the men refused, shot their commander, and joined the civilian protests. Other regiments soon followed their example. Workers had no difficulty seizing some 40,000 rifles from the barracks, turning the demonstrators into a force that could put up a robust defense against attacks by police and soldiers still loyal to the government.

Violence was kept to a minimum. Although rebellious soldiers and workers went on a rampage, destroying their military barracks as well as the Ministry of the Interior and the headquarters of the Okhrana, relatively little blood was shed. The total number of casualties has been estimated at somewhere between 1,300 and 1,450, and of these about 169 died. The government's support had simply evaporated, a development that distinguishes 1917 from 1905. V. V. Shulgin, a conservative deputy in the Duma, accurately described conditions in Petrograd: 'The trouble was that in that large city it was impossible to find a few hundred people who felt kindly toward the Government. There was not a single Minister who believed in himself or in what he was doing.'

Revolutionaries' Pseudonyms

Leading Russian revolutionaries often changed their names, to confuse and evade the police who tried to keep track of them in order to arrest them quickly at times of political unrest. Lenin was born Vladimir Ilych Ulyanov. He adopted the new name in 1901, after exile in Siberia, where he seems to have admired the river Lena, which flows into the Lapten Sea.

Leon Trotsky, the second most prominent leader of the Soviet Union from 1917 until Lenin's death in 1924, was born Lev Davidovich Bronshtein, which clearly identified him as a Jew. No doubt, he had good reason to wish to evade the police, but he may also have wanted to deflect attention from his religious background. When as an adult he was asked about his ethnic background, he replied, 'I am a revolutionary.'

Interestingly, Joseph Stalin was the only top leader of Bolshevism to adopt a name that reflected his personality and aspirations. He was born in Georgia and named Joseph Vissarionovich Dzhugashvili. After Dzugashvili became active in radical politics in 1898, he changed his last name to Stalin, which means 'man of steel'—the embodiment of his conduct and demeanor as dictator of the Soviet Union from 1928 to 1953.

In the meantime (on 27 February), V. M. Rodzianko, an Octobrist who was President of the Duma, sent the Tsar, then on his train in Pskov, a wire warning him that the situation in the capital was precarious and urging him to lose no time in promulgating a series of reforms. 'Tomorrow,' Rodzianko warned, 'will be too late.' Nicholas turned to the Court Chamberlain and uttered the following words: 'That fat Rodzianko has written me some nonsense, to which I shall not even reply.' Nicholas was clearly in denial, because the only step he could think of was to prorogue the Duma. The deputies voted to obey the monarch's order, but they remained in the Duma building and organized an unofficial committee to establish order in the country by reaching out to restless citizens and leaders of public institutions. It was clear to them that the Tsar, having lost the confidence of the people, could no longer govern.

On the same day, two leaders of the Central Workers' Group (K. A. Gvozdev and B. O. Bogdanov), who had just been freed from prison by insurgents, called for the immediate election by workers and others of representatives to a meeting that evening to organize a soviet, which would soon play a critical role in national affairs. Somewhere between forty and fifty people eligible to vote showed up, and elected a Provisional Executive Committee (*Ispolkom*) of eight or nine people, mostly Mensheviks. N. S. Chkheidze was elected as Chairman, and M. I. Skobelev and A. F. Kerensky as his deputies. On 28 February, elections were held for the soviet in factories in Petrograd and military units stationed in the capital. Most of the five thousand chosen representatives belonged to one or another moderate socialist party, but so large a body could not function effectively. Consequently, the Ispolkom, which consisted mainly of intellectuals, ran the affairs of the Petrograd soviet, which also met frequently and had to approve all measures before they could be taken as the policy of the new institution. Initially, the Petrograd soviet focused on practical matters such as forming patrols to maintain order in the streets and providing food for hungry soldiers. Large numbers of workers and soldiers visited the soviet and the Duma to let members of both institutions know that they looked to them for leadership.

The leaders of the Duma sent a delegation to the Tsar, to ask him to resign in favor of his brother, Grand Duke Michael, who would act as regent until a constitutional system of government was created. Many Duma deputies were eager to keep a member of the royal family at the helm of the state to assure an orderly transition to the new order. But Michael indicated that he would accept the crown only from a constitutional assembly elected by the people. Nicholas finally realized that he had lost control over the country; the last straw was the requests from one general after another that he give up the throne for the good of the country. They told him that so long as he ruled, the war could not be won. On 2 March, he abdicated. He wanted to move to Britain, where he had been offered asylum by Lloyd George's government. However, King George V vetoed the invitation, because he feared that the presence of the Russian royal family would provoke major unrest. The Provisional Government then moved Nicholas and his family to the Alexander Palace in Tsarskoe Selo, where they lived for a time, guarded by soldiers loyal to the new government. Soon, the royal family was transferred to the Governor's Mansion in Tobolsk, and then confined to the Ipatiev House in Ekaterinburg, where the entire family was murdered, on the orders of the Bolshevik government, during the night of 16/17 July 1918. The news of the killings was greeted by most people, especially in the cities, with indifference. Karl von Bothmer, the military attaché to the German diplomatic mission in Russia, speculated that the masses had suffered so much ever since the start of the revolution, about one and a half years earlier, that they could not muster any sympathy even for the Tsar, who had claimed to be their little father.

4

The Provisional Government

Long before that bloodletting, soon after the Tsar's abdication, the Duma leadership had settled on a provisional government led by Prince G. E. Lvov, a Kadet who was well regarded because of his extensive work with charitable organizations and service as Chairman of the All-Russian Union of Zemstvos. By all accounts, he was well-meaning and eager to serve his country, but unfortunately for Russia he lacked the attributes of leadership; he was neither charismatic nor interested in making the critical decisions that were needed to calm the people and stabilize the nation after the turbulence of the revolution. Despite the various public positions he had occupied, his experience in administrative work was minimal; he did not consider this a drawback, because he had great faith in the 'sagacity and good will of the people.' But he had no confidence in the central government's ability to solve any of the problems it faced. One of his first statements on assuming the office of Prime Minister was so insipid that it is surprising that he lasted in the highest office in the land as long as he did, about four months. 'The process of the Great Revolution,' he declared, 'is not yet completed, yet each day that we live through strengthens our faith in the inexhaustible power of the Russian people, its political wisdom, the greatness of its soul.' It was widely believed that Miliukov, the most powerful person in the Kadet Party, had pressed Lvov's candidacy for Prime Minister because he knew the prince would be a figurehead and that he—Miliukov—would become the 'power behind the throne.' Miliukov assumed the critical position of Foreign Minister and after considerable wrangling between the liberals and the soviet, one socialist, Alexander Kerensky, joined the cabinet as Minister of Justice. The government could thus claim to be a genuine coalition representing different points of view.

In one of its first actions, the Provisional Government issued its program, which seemed to augur well for the emergence of a democratic Russia. It extended amnesty to all citizens imprisoned for political or religious reasons. It guaranteed freedom of speech and unionization, and legalized strikes, and promised to abolish all restrictions based on social, religious, or national criteria. The government assured the nation that it would remain in power only until a constituent assembly, expected to meet on 30 September and to be elected on the basis of universal, direct, equal, and secret vote, had decided on a constitution and on the form of government for the country. The question of how to deal with the distribution of the land—the most pressing demand of the peasants, by far the largest social group in the country—would be examined immediately, but the final solution of that problem was to be left to the assembly. The government promised to take some measures before then to improve conditions of the poorer peasants.

It was a promising beginning, but it soon became clear that the road to democracy would not be smooth. The Petrograd soviet, which could count on popular support, quickly became a powerful voice of the Left, and its influence grew dramatically once the leaders of the various socialist movements returned from exile. Several were strong personalities, with wide influence in radical circles. Unsurprisingly, it did not take long for the soviet to clash with the Provisional Government over several major issues. The most controversial pertained to the continuation of the war against the Central Powers of Germany,

Austria-Hungary, Bulgaria, and the Ottoman Empire. The Left denounced the conflict as imperialistic and called for an immediate peace 'without annexations and indemnities on the basis of self-determination of peoples.' Miliukov, however, championed continuation of the war. As already noted, he was the most influential member of the government; he claimed that Russia could not abandon its allies, but he also made no effort to conceal his determination to gain control over Constantinople and the straits. The opposition to him in left-wing circles became so intense that in May he had to resign.

Kerensky now became the dominant figure in the government. Only thirty-six years old, he had distinguished himself as a lawyer and gained a national reputation as a defender of several revolutionaries charged with political crimes, and of M. M. Beilis, a Jew accused in 1913 of ritual murder. Kerensky was a man of the Left and had joined the party of the Trudoviki, who were somewhat more moderate than the Socialist Revolutionaries. His success as a lawyer seems to have gone to his head, and he nurtured great ambitions. He was a fiery orator who, according to the British journalist C. A. Wilson, in Petrograd in 1917, succeeded, at least for a few weeks, in inspiring the troops with his rhetoric:

> Crowds gathered for hours to catch a glimpse of him. His path was everywhere strewn with flowers. Soldiers ran for miles after his motor car, trying to shake his hand or kiss the hem of his garment. At his meetings in the great halls of Moscow the audiences worked themselves up into paroxysms of enthusiasm and adoration.

In contrast to most of his left-wing colleagues, Kerensky was no less eager than Miliukov to pursue military victories against the Central Powers but the Petrograd soviet became such a powerful political force that on the most important issues the government could not afford to adopt policies that ran counter to its wishes. On several occasions, the soviet acted entirely on its own, trespassing on the authority of the government even in military matters. The most dramatic and potentially most harmful example was the soviet's issuance, on 1 March, of Order Number 1. Although addressed to the 'Garrison of the Petrograd Military District,' it was quickly assumed to be directed at all the armed forces. It called on soldiers to elect committees that would obey the soviet and to maintain control over all weapons—specifically, not to turn them over to officers. Furthermore, it advised soldiers to follow the orders of their officers and the Provisional Government, but only to the extent that they did not conflict with those of the soviet. Finally, Order Number 1 urged soldiers not to salute officers when off duty and warned officers not to treat men harshly. Clearly, the soviet had arrogated to itself powers normally exercised by the government, and it soon became evident that a novel system of power existed in Russia, which came to be known as *dvoevlastie*, or 'dual power.' A. I. Guchkov, the Minister of War at the time, was appalled and claimed (on 9 March) that the 'Provisional Government exists only so long as it is permitted to do so by the Soviet of Workers' and Soldiers' Deputies. In particular, in the military department, it is possible at present to issue only such orders as basically do not contradict the decision of the above-mentioned Soviet.'

Lenin returns to Russia

It was an arrangement that undermined stability and it could not be tolerated for long. Neither the government nor the soviet boasted a leader of sufficient stature, willpower, and daring to attempt a decisive blow against the other side. Lenin, in Switzerland, was eager to return to Russia to support his Bolshevik colleagues, but a glance at the map will reveal the difficulties he faced; either he would have to cross a country at war with his own country, or he would have to travel via France, which would involve a long delay in reaching his homeland. In any case, France would not be eager to send an influential radical opposed to the war to its ally at a time of turmoil. After some hesitation, several senior German officials concluded that it would be to their advantage to have him and a few dozen other socialists in Russia cross their country to reach Russia, where they could stir up trouble and press the authorities to sue for peace; this diversion from the war would give the Central Powers the opportunity to concentrate on defeating the Western powers. To avoid the charge of dealing with the enemy, Lenin insisted that the train on which he traveled be granted the rights of extraterritoriality and that there be no passport controls. Swiss socialists made the final arrangements for Lenin, and he and thirty-one other exiles of various socialist persuasions crossed Germany into Sweden and from there to Petrograd.

On his arrival in the Russian capital on 3 April, Lenin discovered, to his dismay, that even the leaders of his own party (including, incidentally, Joseph Stalin) favored a policy of conditional support for the new regime, although they were trying to apply pressure to extricate Russia from the war. Rejecting this approach as totally misguided, Lenin demanded that his colleagues adopt a radically different stance. His program was presented in detail in the so-called 'April Theses' that were issued soon after his arrival in Petrograd. The Theses denounced the imperialist war, which, Lenin insisted, could be ended only after the overthrow of capitalism, and they called on soldiers at the front to fraternize with the enemy to prepare the way for peace. The Theses also urged that support for the Provisional Government be ended and that preparations be made for the assumption of power by the soviet. As he put it, 'the country is passing from the first stage of the revolution to its second stage, which must place power in the hands of the proletariat and the poorest sectors of the peasants.'

Finally, the Theses committed the revolutionary government, as soon as it took power, to nationalize the large estates, the vast majority of which belonged to the nobility, and to hand over the land to the Soviets of Farmhands Deputies, which would ensure that a new agrarian policy was adopted for the benefit of the peasantry.

In his 'First Letter on Tactics,' published in late April, Lenin acknowledged that his proposals seemed to violate the Marxist doctrine that the working class should take over the government only after control was held by the bourgeoisie and a capitalist economic system established. In a striking confession of opportunism, or pragmatism—which word is chosen depends on one's political convictions—he declared that 'theory, my friend, is grey, but green is the eternal tree of life.' One must not, he continued, 'sacrifice living Marxism to a dead letter.' In any case, the working class in Russia would seize power together with the peasants, who were also part of the bourgeoisie. A seizure of power in collaboration with the peasantry therefore could be construed as a step toward 'completing' the bourgeois-democratic revolution, 'Why,' asked Lenin, 'should this be impossible?'

Even his closest colleagues in the Bolshevik Party found Lenin's scheme fantastic, and many wondered whether their leader had lost touch with reality, but he was not easily dissuaded and worked diligently to convince party members that his strategy was based on a realistic analysis of conditions in the Russian Empire. He completed a long essay, 'State and Revolution. The Marxist Theory of the State and the Tasks of the Proletariat in the Revolution,' in which he went to great pains to demonstrate that he had by no means abandoned Marxism. It also demonstrated that he was a very complicated political activist: despite the hard-headed strategy and tactics he had proposed for the seizure of power by the proletariat, he remained a starry-eyed utopian, whose plans for Russia amounted to nothing less than a perfect society on earth, the kind of society that John Reed, the

American journalist reporting on events in Russia in 1917, found so appealing.

Actually, Lenin had written much of 'State and Revolution' before the upheaval of 1917, at a time when he was pessimistic about living long enough to witness the triumph of socialism. The work has often been dismissed as an aberration totally unrepresentative of his convictions, but in fact it accurately conveys a streak in his thinking that can also be discerned in his writings of the 1890s and 1918. The utopian impulse was part of his psychological make-up and seems always to have been a part of his political vision. Readers who keep this characteristic in mind will find it easier to understand his strategy and tactics from 1917 until his death in 1924.

Basing himself on Marx, Lenin postulated a traditional two-stage development by Russia toward the final goal of a classless society, although he was not precise in delineating between the bourgeois and the proletarian phases, apparently because the first would gradually grow into the second. After the destruction of bourgeois parliamentarism, the victorious proletariat would establish a democratic republic modeled on the Paris Commune of 1871. The standing army would be abolished, and functionaries would cease to act like 'bureaucrats' or 'officials' and would be subject to recall at any time. Their salaries would be no larger than that of the average worker, and parliamentary institutions would be replaced by 'working bodies, executive and legislative at the same time.' Private ownership of production would, of course, be eliminated. Once resistance to the new order is overcome, 'the state ... ceases to exist' and 'it becomes possible to speak of freedom':

> [Under] communism people will gradually become accustomed to observing the elementary rules of social intercourse that have been known for centuries and repeated for thousands of years in all copybook maxims.

They will become accustomed to observing them without force, without coercion, without subordination, without the special apparatus for coercion called the state.

All citizens would be employees of the state; the 'accounting and control' necessary to administer the functions of society would be so simplified that any 'literate person' would be able to perform them; all he would need was a 'knowledge of the four rules of arithmetic, and [of] issuing appropriate receipts.' Several times in the essay, Lenin categorically denied that he was a utopian dreamer unaware of human failings. On the contrary, he acknowledged that during the initial period of the new order some citizens might indulge in excesses and might violate the 'rules of social intercourse,' but he was certain that the culprits would be stopped without recourse to a 'special apparatus of suppression.' The initiative would be taken 'by the armed people themselves, as simply and as readily as any crowd of civilized people, even in modern society, interfere to put a stop to a scuffle or to prevent a woman from being assaulted.' Eventually, the 'excesses will inevitably begin to *wither away.*' Lenin could say this with utter confidence because he believed that the source of all evil, exploitation, would have been extinguished; everyone would receive from society 'as much as he has given to it. Equality apparently reigns supreme.'

That a hardheaded person such as Lenin, who prided himself on his rationality and made a point of dismissing wishful thinking of every kind, could spout such romantic views is puzzling. But a close study of his personality is not easy because—like the eminent revolutionary Robespierre—he went to great lengths to suppress his emotions. We now know that he was highly complex and moved by radically different impulses. One such impulse was rage, which clearly affected many of his judgments and actions. How else can we explain his intemperate denunciations of capitalism and bourgeois society? Not content with pointing out their economic and social inequities, he condemned the capitalist system as a 'slave society, since the "free" workers, who all their life work for the capitalists, are "entitled" only to such means of subsistence as are essential for the maintenance of slaves who produce profit, for the safeguarding and perpetuation of capitalist slavery.' Proletarian democracy, he asserted on another occasion, was a *million times* more democratic than any bourgeois democracy. Indeed, '[the] more highly developed a [bourgeois] democracy is, the more imminent are pogroms or civil war in connection with any profound divergence which is dangerous to the bourgeoisie.'

That Lenin was at times consumed with rage is also suggested by his mode of writing, which was polemical in the extreme. He quoted his opponents often and at great length, and then heaped abuse on them without ever responding to the substance of their arguments. Thus, after breaking with Karl Kautsky, whom he had revered for many years as the great theorist of socialism, Lenin denounced him for expressing disapproval of Bolshevik violations of democracy as a 'Marxist in words and a lackey of the bourgeoisie in deeds,' as a 'reactionary, an enemy of the working class, a henchman of the bourgeoisie,' as 'our revolutionary Judas Kautsky.' On the inside cover of a book he owned, Lenin wrote that 'out of every hundred Bolsheviks, seventy are fools and twenty-nine rogues, and only one a real socialist.' Frequently, he referred to 'vulgar, stinking liberalism' and dismissed those he disagreed with as 'windbags,' 'opportunists,' 'rogues,' 'scoundrels,' 'liars,' 'swine,' or 'poseurs.' In conversations with colleagues, he would deliver tirades against his enemies during which he could barely control his attacks on those who disagreed with him. Invariably, his outbursts exhausted him and plunged him into listlessness and depression. It was his wife, Krupskaia, who first attributed Lenin's frenzied and reckless attacks on all who in any way challenged him to his 'rage.'

His inner rage expressed itself most dramatically in his penchant for violence. 'Major questions in the life of nations,' he contended more than once, 'are settled only by force.' He defended revolutionary violence as a legitimate response to the violence of 'reactionary classes,' but his advocacy of forceful measures was actually much broader than this argument suggests. In a private letter of 11 February 1905, Lenin denounced comrades who had hesitated to organize circles in Russia to promote the Bolshevik cause, and then called for their physical elimination:

> I am for shooting on the spot anyone [referring to other Bolsheviks] who presumes to say that there are no people to be had [to work for the Bolshevik cause]. The people in Russia are legion; all we have to do is to recruit young people more widely and boldly, more boldly and widely, and again more widely and again more boldly … This is a time of war.

By contrast, as an analyst of the state of affairs in 1917, and as a political tactician, Lenin was a genius. He sensed before anyone else that the Russian Empire was falling apart, giving the Bolsheviks an opening to seize power. In the weeks after Lenin first offered this analysis, developments throughout the country bore out his perspicacity. Shortly after the collapse of tsarism, people in numerous localities took the initiative in forming local councils or soviets that assumed the functions of government in their areas. In the army, discipline broke down as soldiers, in growing numbers, came to view the war as futile; many deserted and went back to their villages to seize land from the landlords. Workers in numerous factories took control after ejecting their supervisors and bosses from the premises. Finally, in some regions—most notably Finland, Ukraine, Lithuania, Latvia, Transcaucasia, and Poland—national movements demanded autonomy or complete separation from the empire.

The peasants rebel

The role of the peasants in the country's social and political disintegration after the collapse of tsarism merits special attention, if for no other reason than that they constituted 80 percent of the population. Despite the activism of the peasants during the Revolution of 1905, there were many within the ruling groups who still did not understand the depth of discontent in the countryside. Most peasants believed fervently that all land belonged to those who worked it and therefore demanded that all the land held by landlords, the state, and the Church should be handed over to them. The liberals and the various socialist parties all favored changes in the system of landholding. Some proposed nationalization of the land, some wished to distribute all land to the peasants, and still others called for more modest changes. In short, the land question was extraordinarily complicated and the discussions over how to proceed promised to be lengthy and contentious.

The peasants were in no mood to wait. They wanted the land issue to be resolved quickly, and since they considered themselves full citizens with the right to play a significant role in shaping the political and legal order of Russia, they increasingly took matters into their own hands. Within weeks of the collapse of tsarism, peasants in many parts of the country formed committees to set the agenda with regard to the land. In certain areas, women, who made up two-thirds of the workforce, because so many men were serving at the front, participated in local committees pressing for rapid change. Returning soldiers were another potent force in supporting peasant demands. It did not take long for peasant dissatisfaction to spill over into direct action to bring about change. Such a turn of events was not unprecedented; between 1910 and 1914 there were 17,000 incidents of peasant unrest in the European areas of Russia alone. In 1917, peasants resorted to direct action on a far greater scale.

The Provisional Government was incapable of stopping any of these mass movements. To complicate matters, it vigorously pursued policies—such as continuation of the war—that provoked a new round of street demonstrations. Foreign Minister Miliukov, after refusing to renounce his support for Russia's annexationist aims in the war, was disavowed by the Provisional Government and, as noted above, by early May he had no choice but to resign. At about the same time, Guchkov, the Minister of War, followed suit, for reasons already mentioned. In the reconstituted government, six of fifteen ministers were socialists, which led some to believe that it would now be possible to find common ground with the soviet, but it soon became evident that on some issues the government would be riven by strife and that on others it would adopt policies not very different from those of the previous one. On 7 July, Lvov resigned because he considered the new government's policies too radical. He was replaced by Kerensky, who, despite being a leftist, believed that he could rally the troops and lead them to victory against the Central Powers. The radical Left came to despise him, as is indicated by Trotsky's sneering description of his attempt to encourage the fighting forces:

> Kerensky toured the front, adjured and threatened the troops, kneeled, kissed the earth—in a word, clowned it in every possible way, while he failed to answer any of the questions tormenting the soldiers. He had deceived himself by his cheap effects, and assured of the support of the congress of Soviets, ordered the offensive.

Early in July, the army went on the offensive against the Germans. Initially, it scored some victories, but as soon as it encountered stiff resistance, the weakness of the Russians emerged. Discipline collapsed and they were soon routed. In a desperate attempt to restore discipline, the government reinstituted the death penalty for serious violations of military regulations, but the measure had little effect. Morale could not be revived and discipline could not be restored. At the start of the revolution in March, the army did not want to protect the tsarist order, and four months later many soldiers had lost interest in defending Russia's borders.

The July days

Early in July, a new wave of unrest erupted in Petrograd. To this day, its origins remain controversial, although no one disputes its importance. In his autobiography, Trotsky insisted that the demonstrations were 'spontaneous, at the initiative of the masses.' However, some historians contend that the Bolsheviks instigated the upheaval; they had waged an intense campaign of propaganda among the already radicalized soldiers in support of the party's demand of 'All Power to the Soviets,' and now that demand was especially appealing to disgruntled soldiers and workers. The government's decision to send a sizable number of troops stationed in the capital to the front in preparation for an offensive against the Germans proved to be the spark that set off the unrest, especially since many suspected that the government was eager to rid Petrograd of the soldiers, who were strong supporters of the Bolsheviks. The Leninists had succeeded in making many converts in the First Machine Gun Regiment, which was housed in the Vyborg District, not far from factories with large numbers of radical workers. On the other hand, the most persuasive argument against the claim that the Bolsheviks instigated the July unrest is that Lenin was in Finland at the time, recuperating from a slight illness, and that his followers were unlikely to have initiated a major action without his presence—he was the one indispensable person in the Bolshevik Party.

No one denies that the Bolsheviks played a major role in the upheaval once it had started. On 3 July, soldiers in the local garrison, enraged over worsening economic conditions and the defeats at the front, took to the streets under banners that called on the soviet to take power. Workers quickly joined the movement and by the second day the crowds in the streets were estimated to number around 500,000. The demonstrators, many of whom carried weapons, scuffled with the police and soldiers loyal to the government; when the unrest ended, several scores of people had been killed and over one hundred had been wounded. At the end of the first day, the leaders of the Bolsheviks in Petrograd had officially given their blessing to the action, perhaps because they could not remain aloof from a movement that echoed their own demands that power be ceded to the soviet. It would be odd if such encouragement did not give a boost to the demonstrators.

The Petrograd soviet, dominated by Mensheviks and Socialist Revolutionaries, vainly pleaded with the demonstrators to end the street action. At one point, the Socialist Revolutionary Minister of Agriculture, Chernov, tried to convince a large crowd in the streets of the capital that seizure of power by the soviet at that time was inadvisable, because the country was not prepared for so radical a shift in the political system. The angry demonstrators were not persuaded by his argument; they surrounded him and after searching him, several accused him of being 'one of the people who shoots at the people.' A worker shook his fists and shouted, 'Take the power, you son of a bitch, when it is given to you.' Some members of the crowd then seized the minister and after tearing his coat pushed him into a car and vowed to hold him until the soviet replaced the Provisional Government. Fortunately for Chernov, Trotsky, who was greatly admired by the demonstrators, arrived on the scene and managed to pry the prisoner loose from his captors and bring him back to the Tauride Palace, the building housing the soviet.

The government clamped down on the demonstration by arresting several of its leaders and seeking to take the leaders of some of the radical parties into custody. Several of them, including Lenin, went into hiding, but Trotsky, among others, was jailed and remained in prison for several weeks. Although the uprising had failed in its immediate objective, it had revealed the boldness of the radical movement and put the Provisional Government on notice that its policies had not succeeded in restoring calm.

Most of the news shortly after the July Days, on the economy as well as on the war, continued to be bad, yet one unexpected revelation gave the authorities a ray of hope that they might be able to weather the storm. On 8 July, the sensational, ultraconservative newspaper *Zhivoe slovo* accused the Bolsheviks of having received substantial sums of money from the German government, and claimed that the infusion of foreign gold had enabled the Bolsheviks to wage their campaign against the Provisional Government. The Germans' motive, of course, was to undermine Russia's war effort. Within hours of the appearance of these charges, other newspapers repeated them, some now referring to Lenin as a 'provocateur.' Among the political class, the revelation became the central topic of conversation. Even Plekhanov, the father of Russian Marxism and former ally of Lenin, found the evidence in *Zhivoe slovo* convincing. Lenin and other leading Bolsheviks vehemently denied the charges, but few of his political opponents found those denials persuasive.

The evidence presented at the time was meager, but years later scholars found some documents that give credence to the accusations. The person who helped arrange the transfer of money to the Bolsheviks is now widely accepted to have been Parvus, the socialist who first advanced the 'theory of permanent revolution.' Parvus was intelligent and clever, but he was also an adventurer and intriguer with few scruples about how he pursued his political goals. He had convinced himself that by means of his own self-aggrandizement he would be able to advance the cause of socialism. Moreover, unlike most radicals of his generation, Parvus was not content to restrict himself to politics; he wanted to live the good life as well as influence the course of history, both of which he thought he could do by amassing a fortune. Hence, he engaged in economic speculation and cultivated high government officials in various countries; by 1914, while only in his forties, he had demonstrated exceptional skill in both endeavors, which was enough to raise eyebrows among his socialist colleagues. He came to be known as a socialist tycoon, and his behavior resembled the Marxist caricature of capitalists. When he went to Zurich in 1915, for example, he stayed at the most luxurious hotel, was almost always surrounded by corpulent blonde women, and revealed a penchant for big, expensive cigars and champagne. By the time of his death in 1924, Parvus had led so variegated a career that he was reputed to have been, at one and the same time, a speculator, swindler, Turkish agent, Russian agent, lackey of imperialism, and, above all, traitor to socialism.

Parvus's opportunity to shape the course of history presented itself after the outbreak of World War I. Convinced that Germany, with its powerful labor movement, represented progress and that autocratic Russia embodied black reaction, he immediately set about trying to forge an alliance between the German government and European—especially Russian—socialists. Such a collaboration was called for, he reasoned, because the military defeat of tsarism would unleash the revolution in Russia, which, in turn, would set off a chain of events that would end in the socialist transformation of Germany and eventually Western Europe.

In February 1915, Parvus established close contact with the German Foreign Office, which he persuaded of the soundness of at least one part of his plan: that Russian socialists could help weaken their nation's war effort if they possessed sufficient means to mount a massive propaganda campaign among the masses. As a first instalment, the Foreign Office gave Parvus a million marks, and so began his travels to wherever Russian socialists were to be found. At their meetings, he argued political issues with them and lavished funds on them, secure in the conviction that money was a potent political weapon. He also spent a considerable amount of time in Berlin, where he was several times received by dignitaries, who listened to him with great respect and passed his thoughts on to the Chancellor, Theobald von Bethmann-Hollweg. The safe conduct through Germany granted to Lenin in 1917, and the money given to the Bolsheviks that year, were the logical culmination of this bizarre sequence of events. Notably, a document drafted on 23 August (commonly noted as 5 September in the Gregorian calendar) 1917, by Minister of Foreign Affairs Baron R. von Kühlmann, which was discovered after World War II, indicates that the Bolsheviks 'received from us a steady flow of funds through various channels and under varying labels.' Thus, Parvus served Bolshevism not only as a theorist but also in more practical ways.

How much money the Bolsheviks received from Germany is not known and it is therefore impossible to gauge its impact. However, it would probably be a mistake to conclude that the Bolsheviks would not have succeeded in seizing power without it. The charge leveled at Lenin that he was a 'German agent' is not tenable. He acted as he did because he believed in the desirability and necessity of a Bolshevik revolution. He succeeded, primarily because of the dreadful conditions in Russia and the innumerable missteps of the men who took over the government after the abdication of Tsar Nicholas II.

Democracy endangered: the Kornilov affair

Two months after the July Days, the Provisional Government suffered its most serious blow during a series of strange events that later came to be known as the Kornilov Affair. This blow was delivered not by the Left but by conservatives who had concluded that Kerensky was not capable of restoring stability to Russia. Kerensky, for his part, made one mistake after another in dealing with the challenge from the Right, which undermined his position among liberals and moderate socialists and sealed the fate of the attempt to steer Russia along a democratic path. The affair is also important because it sheds light on the type of leaders—self-serving, adventurous, and even reckless—that had reached the heights of power.

At the beginning of September, it appeared as though the Provisional Government might be able to weather the revolutionary storm. The insurrection of early July had been suppressed, the most important Bolshevik leaders were either in prison or in hiding, the agrarian disturbances had subsided, and a government committee was studying the explosive land question. There were even some signs that the military situation was improving. It seemed that the army might succeed in reestablishing some semblance of discipline in its ranks. More importantly, American troops were arriving in France in growing numbers and their presence, it was thought, would decrease German pressure on the Eastern Front and give the Russian army more time to recover from its defeats and internal turmoil. There was growing optimism that if the government could hold out until the Constituent Assembly met and produced a progressive constitution, the liberal democratic aspirations of the revolution might still be realized.

The unexpected Kornilov rebellion of 27 August undermined the delicate political stability that prevailed in Russia. It aroused fears of counterrevolution and raised new questions about the ability of Kerensky, who had been appointed Prime Minister when Lvov resigned on 20 July, to preserve the gains of the revolution. In political circles, Kerensky was even suspected of having conspired with General Kornilov to enhance his own power. The turmoil that gripped the country revitalized the Left and particularly the Bolsheviks, who exploited the fear that the Right would return to power. Two years after going into exile,

Kerensky correctly referred to the Kornilov Affair as the 'prelude to Bolshevism,' but because of its complexity, some aspects of the affair still remain unclear.

With good reason, Kerensky had concluded in the summer of 1917 that a major weakness of his government was the lack of support by an assembly representative of the people. Such support, it was generally assumed, would be provided by the Constituent Assembly, but it proved difficult to organize a national election quickly, and hence the voting was postponed several times. Kerensky, therefore, conceived of a way to demonstrate right away that the Russian people supported the government; he would summon a State Conference to be held in Moscow for three days in mid-August. The government made an effort to achieve a balance between the Right and Left among the 2,414 delegates by including in the conference representatives of the trade unions, cooperatives, and soviets; but the moderates and conservatives, who comprised members of the four Dumas, the representatives from the army, the universities, the liberal professions, and various associations of landowners, exceeded their proportion of the population at large. Consequently, the conference was unlikely to be looked upon with favor by the masses, who now played a crucial role in national affairs.

To enhance the prestige of the conference and to demonstrate the wide support for his government, Kerensky invited the Commander in Chief, General Lavr Georgevich Kornilov, to address the delegates. It was one of his greatest mistakes as Prime Minister. Although Kerensky had appointed Kornilov to the highest position in the armed forces during the grave military crisis that followed the collapse of the July upheaval, the general was not the type of person to be forever grateful for the promotion. He had his own agenda and, perhaps more importantly, he had his own ambitions, which were boundless. One of his virtues, in Kerensky's view, was his greater receptivity to liberal tendencies than his military colleagues. Moreover, Kerensky considered

Kornilov a more effective commander than General A.A. Brusilov, who did not have the personal qualities to inspire the troops to carry out orders issued by officers. Kornilov had gained a legendary reputation for his dramatic escape from Austrian captivity in 1916. During the early days of the revolution in February 1917, he had further endeared himself to the Provisional Government with his criticism of the Petrograd Soviet, which, he charged, exercised more authority over the troops than the generals.

Kerensky's promotion of Kornilov to the post of Commander-in-Chief was a bold but risky decision by the Prime Minister, because in matters political the new leader of the armed forces showed astonishing naïveté. He lacked the ability to express himself diplomatically, and his unrestrained language invariably offended officials. He relied heavily on his public relations official, V. S. Zavoiko, who played a sinister role throughout the affair and formulated Kornilov's views and requests in provocative language. Patriotic to the core, brave, disinterested in personal wealth, unconcerned for his own safety, Kornilov aimed above all at revitalizing Russia's fighting force. However, to achieve his aim he could not avoid involvement in politics, an area about which he was amazingly ignorant. For example, he did not understand that there were crucial differences between the relatively moderate socialists, who were dominant in the soviets, and the Bolsheviks.

That the world of politics was alien to him became evident when he indicated that he would accept the post of Supreme Commander only under the following extraordinary conditions: that he would retain responsibility to his own conscience and to the people at large; that he would be given absolute freedom in the issuance of field orders and in the appointment of senior commanders; and that the death penalty would be reintroduced wherever army units were stationed, not merely at the front. In short, he did not accept the principle that the military was subordinate to the country's political leaders. Surprisingly, Kerensky seems to have accepted the 'substance' of Kornilov's conditions, although he vigorously objected to the 'ultimative manner' in which they were presented.

Inevitably, several squabbles arose between Kornilov and Kerensky over appointments and other matters, but they were able to settle their differences because they concurred on two essential points: they wanted to reestablish discipline in the army and order in the country. Both also considered the other necessary to attain these goals. Kerensky had the requisite political experience and public support; Kornilov the military. However, the meteoric rise of Kornilov's popularity, and the frequent rumors of imminent *coups*, prompted Kerensky to view the general as a dangerous rival. Kornilov developed a hearty dislike for the Prime Minister, who struck him as an eternal talker who accomplished little.

The tension between Kerensky and Kornilov became evident to the public in mid-August, when both men appeared at the Moscow State Conference. Contrary to the Prime Minister's plans, the conference quickly revealed that it would not provide the government with the support he had hoped for. Instead of serving as a rallying point for national unity, the gathering tended to bring into even sharper relief the unbridgeable cleavage that divided Russian society. When Kerensky appeared on the podium, the Left and some moderates rose and cheered; the right side of the hall remained seated and silent. On Kornilov's entry, the Right accorded him a resounding ovation, while Kerensky's—more numerous—supporters remained silent.

It had already been apparent on 13 August, when Kornilov arrived in Moscow, that many Russians looked to him as their potential savior. There is considerable evidence that members of important business circles in Petrograd and Moscow had been organizing on his behalf for some time, and that they had carefully planned a boisterous reception. As he entered the city, flowers littered the railway station. Crowds of citizens and soldiers lined the streets to catch a glimpse of the hero. A guard of honor composed of officers from the Alexander Military School stood smartly at attention. Various other officers' organizations sent greetings. A military band played stirring music as Kornilov made his first appearance surrounded by his picturesquely attired Caucasian soldiers. While officers carried Kornilov to the people on their shoulders, a portrait and biography of the hero were widely scattered from automobiles. F. I. Rodichev, a leading Kadet, ended his short address of welcome with the provocative words: 'Save Russia, and a grateful people will reward you!'

In his opening remarks, Kerensky delivered a vague and fiery speech in which he threatened to put down 'with blood and iron' all attempts to overthrow the government, a threat aimed at both Kornilov and the Bolsheviks. General Kornilov's address dealt with more concrete issues. After painting the condition of the army and the situation at the front in the bleakest colors, he called for the creation of an army based on 'iron discipline' in which the prestige of the officers would be restored. He also urged the government to take steps, no matter how harsh, to assure the army of an adequate supply of goods. The Right applauded enthusiastically.

Unexpectedly, the State Conference ended on a conciliatory note. I. G. Tsereteli, a Menshevik and leading spokesman for the Left, and A. A. Bublikov, a leading spokesman for industrial Russia, shook hands on the stage of the Bolshoi Theatre. This gesture was meant to symbolize the unity of the nation, 'the armistice between capital and labor in the name of struggle for Russia.' In reality, as the British Ambassador to Russia pointed out, the conference accentuated the differences between the various parties. A new governmental crisis was generally expected within a few weeks. Rumors about possible *coups d'état* were rampant.

Kerensky became increasingly suspicious that a plan was afoot to unseat him. After returning to Petrograd, he told B. V. Savinkov, an adventurer, at one time a revolutionary terrorist, and now the Prime Minister's right-hand man on military affairs, that at the Moscow State Conference 'the Counterrevolution had raised its head.' He was convinced that a diverse group of right-wing conspirators had found a leader around whom they could coalesce: General Kornilov. Which organizations and individuals lent him their active support was still not clear, although it was generally assumed that he could count on General A. S. Lukomsky, his chief of staff. It is now also fairly well established that the League of Officers of the Army and Navy was plotting both in Petrograd and at the Stavka (general headquarters of the armed forces). In addition, suspicion centered on the Council of the Cossack Troops League, which at the time of the Moscow Conference had asserted that 'General Kornilov cannot be removed.' Other right-wing groups had issued similar statements.

Although knowledge of the preparations for a plot against Kerensky is still hazy, we know that by late in August military plans had been worked out. On 20 August, an officer arrived at Berdichev with a personal message from Kornilov to General Denikin. It referred to 'reliable information' that the Bolsheviks planned 'a rising' in the capital within a few days. The Third Cavalry Corps had been sent to Petrograd with orders to 'crush the uprising, and simultaneously put an end to the soviets.' Once that objective was achieved, Petrograd was to be declared in a state of war and a new Kornilov Program (content unknown) would be published. Denikin was asked to send a score or more of reliable officers to the capital, where they would be held in readiness for action against an uprising. On 21 August, Quartermaster-General I. P. Romanovsky ordered the distribution of hand grenades to three cavalry units, which were to surround and occupy Petrograd from the south.

At a crucial moment, the Commander-in-Chief received what must have appeared to him as a curious, though welcome, order. On 23 August, Savinkov arrived at the Stavka with a special request from Kerensky. Kornilov was now thoroughly disgusted with the Prime Minister's indecisiveness and failure to effect any far-reaching measures to restore order and economic efficiency.

The general's mood changed considerably when Savinkov informed him that Kerensky had decided to reestablish capital punishment in areas not directly in the war zone. Furthermore, Savinkov passed on to Kornilov the following additional requests: First, the general was to send the Union of Officers, a certain number of whom were suspected of participating in an anti-government conspiracy, to Moscow, where, Kerensky believed, they would be isolated and thus not in a position to pursue their political goal. Second, Kornilov was to liquidate the political department attached to the Stavka, for the same reason. Third, Kornilov was to send a cavalry corps to Petrograd, to be placed at the government's disposal. In issuing the third order, Kerensky played right into Kornilov's hands by moving anti-government troops to the capital.

Strange and confusing as the events of this affair had been up to this point, the most mysterious and bizarre were yet to take place. They are noteworthy because they provide another glimpse into the amateurishness of the country's leaders, which was probably a consequence of the Tsars' retention of political power in their hands, which prevented educated citizens from acquiring political experience. On 22 August, the former Procurator of the Holy Synod, V. N. Lvov (not related to the former prime minister) visited Kerensky at the Winter Palace. Posing as the spokesman of important social groups, Lvov offered free advice to the Prime Minister. He told Kerensky that the Provisional Government had lost support among both the Right and the democratic elements. Only by changing its composition could the government be effective. Lvov suggested that elements more moderate than the Kadets needed to be given senior positions. When Kerensky asked Lvov to specify exactly which forces he represented, the latter merely answered that he was backed by a 'considerable force' and that he had been instructed to find out whether the Prime Minister was willing to reconstitute the government.

Lvov then proceeded to the Stavka and posed as the fully-empowered emissary of Kerensky. Exactly what Lvov said to Kornilov is not clear, but he seems to have intimated that the government was amenable to the idea of a dictatorship. Kerensky, according to Lvov, was considering three possibilities: the establishment of a new government with himself as dictator; the creation of a new government with unlimited powers, consisting of three or five members, one of whom would be Kornilov; or the appointment of Kornilov as dictator and Supreme Commander of the armed forces. Which of these options, asked Lvov, would the general prefer? Kornilov, elated at Kerensky's willingness to capitulate peacefully, expressed his approval of the third. The general also asked that Kerensky declare martial law in Petrograd and suggested that both the Prime Minister and Savinkov come to the Stavka, as their safety could not be guaranteed in the capital. The composition of the new government was then freely discussed at headquarters, and it was generally assumed that Kerensky would be named Minister of Justice and Savinkov Minister of War. However, during a conversation with V. S. Zavoiko, Kornilov's man in charge of public relations, Lvov became convinced that plans were being hatched to assassinate Kerensky.

Lvov hurried to the capital for a second interview with the Prime Minister on the evening of 26 August. When Kerensky learned of Kornilov's intentions, he was taken aback, and his first thought was to verify Lvov's message. The affair now took a turn that can only be characterized as bizarre.

After Lvov left his office, Kerensky called Kornilov on the Hughes apparatus (a kind of teletype machine) and impersonated Lvov. He asked the general to confirm the message sent to the Prime Minister. Kerensky, still speaking as Lvov, indicated that the Prime Minister wanted personal confirmation because he did not fully trust Lvov. Kornilov confirmed that Lvov had forwarded his message correctly. At that point, Kerensky identified himself and indicated that he now understood that Lvov had correctly passed Kornilov's message on to him. The Prime Minister said he would leave for headquarters the next day. It was a brief conversation and there is some question whether either fully understood what the other was saying. Amazingly, Lvov, a man with no authority to conduct high-level negotiations, figured prominently in bringing down the Provisional Government.

Shortly after this conversation on the teletype, Lvov returned to Kerensky's office to warn the Prime Minister that it would be dangerous for him to go to the Stavka. At that point, Kerensky ordered Lvov's arrest and decided to deal swiftly with the impending threat to his authority.

At 4 a.m. on 27 August, Kerensky met with his cabinet, which quickly conferred upon him unlimited power to deal with the crisis. Kerensky rejected Savinkov's advice to negotiate directly with Kornilov as well as Miliukov's and General Alekseev's offers to go to military headquarters as mediators. Instead, he sent a message to Kornilov dismissing him as Commander-in-Chief and directing him to hand over his office to General Lukomsky. He also ordered Kornilov to come immediately to Petrograd.

As news of these developments spread, fear gripped the capital. In violation of his promise, Kornilov had appointed General A. M. Krymov commander of the Savage Division, known for its ruthlessness, and ordered him to advance toward the capital, where the Bolsheviks were rumored to be planning an uprising. Petrograd seemed defenseless and many believed that a bloodbath was imminent.

To everyone's surprise, Kornilov's rebellion ended without the spilling of a single drop of blood. General Kornilov had not reckoned with the listlessness of his troops, or with the vigorous opposition of the workers. The soviet, controlled by a non-Bolshevik majority, immediately organized workers for defense against the counterrevolution. 'The Soviet,' Chernov wrote, 'did not waste time on words, but acted as it had in the best days of the Revolution.' It formed a 'Committee for Struggle with Counterrevolution,' composed of a wide range of representatives from political parties and trade unions, and it was largely as a result of the efforts of this committee, not the government, that the rebellion was quickly quashed.

Especially effective measures were taken by the railway workers who, heeding the advice of the soviet, crippled the lines of communication and transportation. Some army detachments bound for Petrograd were sent in the wrong direction, realizing the error too late. Tracks were blocked with coaches and in three places were torn up, causing endless delays. Continuous streams of agitators visited the soldiers, urging them to disobey orders. The soviet and the Provisional Government bombarded the soldiers with proclamations bearing the same message. Kornilov's declarations rarely reached them. A Moslem delegation organized by the soviet was received by the Savage Division; when informed that there had been no Bolshevik uprising, many of its soldiers decided to remain loyal to the government. Many others were persuaded by soviet agitators not to move against the Kerensky government, using the simple argument that it had freed soldiers from tsarist tyranny.

With the revolt obviously crumbling, the Prime Minister called on General Alekseev to help him extinguish what was clearly a senseless and harmful mutiny. Alekseev sent a message to General Krymov informing him that there was no Bolshevik uprising in Petrograd; he also asked him to halt the movement of his troops and to report to him in the capital. Krymov entered Petrograd by himself and spoke briefly with Kerensky. The content of the conversation is not known, but shortly after the meeting ended, the general went into the Bureau of the War Office and shot himself. On 1 September, Generals Kornilov and Lukomsky, realizing that their rebellion had turned into a fiasco, resigned and, together with several other officers, they were arrested on orders of General Alekseev.

5
Bolsheviks in power

The Kornilov rebellion was essentially a test of strength between Kornilov, who wished to save Russia from Bolshevism and to conduct a successful war against Germany, and Kerensky, who also wanted to win the war and in addition, turn Russia into a democracy. Each of them believed that he was the only one who could save Russia from the abyss. The victor in this fierce conflict, strange as it may sound, was Lenin. The Bolsheviks had supported the struggle against Kornilov, but not because they supported the Provisional Government. Lenin explained their position in a letter of 30 August to the Central Committee of the Russian Social Democratic Labor Party:

> We will fight, we are fighting against Kornilov, even as Kerensky's troops do, but we do not support Kerensky. On the contrary, we expose his weakness … without renouncing the task of overthrowing Kerensky right now; we shall approach the task of struggling against him in a different way, namely, we shall point out to the people … the *weakness* and *vacillation* of Kerensky. This has been done before. Now, however, it has become the main thing.

At this time, a group of sailors visited Trotsky and asked him, 'Isn't it time to arrest the government?' 'No, not yet,' Trotsky replied.

'Use Kerensky as a gun-rest to shoot Kornilov. Afterward we will settle with Kerensky.'

Militarily, the Bolsheviks benefited from Kornilov's rebellion. In its anxiety to create a fighting force against Kornilov's advancing troops, the Provisional Government had permitted the indiscriminate arming of workers. Many did not return their arms after the rebellion had fizzled out, and this made possible the formation of the first units of the Red Guard under the command of the soviet. Before the revolt, the soviet could count on the support of some self-organized militias. Within a few weeks, the Red Guards numbered 25,000. 'The army that rose against Kornilov,' wrote Trotsky, 'was the army-to-be of the October [November] Revolution.' Although Trotsky was exaggerating somewhat, the nucleus of the Bolshevik armed forces was created at that time.

Perhaps the most far-reaching consequence of the whole affair was the general demoralization. The rank and file of the army lost what little faith they still had in their officers. Furthermore, soldiers demanded that instead of being treated leniently, the generals who had supported the rebellion ought to suffer the same punishment they were so eager to apply to disobedient men in the ranks. 'When it was realized,' Chernov wrote, 'that discipline and capital punishment were for soldiers, not for generals, the front swelled with anger and turned black like the sea before a tempest. The Bolsheviks had only to catch the favoring wind and fill their sails.' A new round of desertions, as well as increasing physical attacks on officers, speeded the disintegration of the tsarist army.

Everywhere, Bolsheviks and right-wingers whispered that Kerensky had been in accord with Kornilov on the necessity of a dictatorship, and that the Prime Minister had betrayed the general only under pressure from the soviets. Inevitably, these charges and revelations undermined the confidence of the masses in the Kerensky government. Furthermore, in the light of the sympathy various liberals (especially Miliukov) had expressed for the Kornilov movement, it became impossible for the centrist parties to continue cooperating in the government. Mutual confidence had disappeared. When the Bolsheviks, after the attempted knockout blow from the Right, countered with their own blow in October, they faced no united opposition.

The Bolsheviks reaped their first concrete advantage from the Kornilov Affair on 25 September. In elections that day, they achieved what they had longed for ever since the revolution in March, a majority in the Petrograd soviet. Five days later, they scored the same success in Moscow. Fear of counterrevolution had produced a decisive shift to the left among the working class; that shift could not but encourage the Bolsheviks in their hopes for a forcible seizure of power. Referring to these electoral victories, Lenin wrote to the Central Committees in Petrograd and Moscow of the Russian Social Democratic Party between 7–9 October:

> Having obtained a majority in the Soviets of Workers' and Soldiers' Deputies of both capitals, the Bolsheviks can and must take power into their hands. Assume power at once in Moscow and in Petrograd (it does not matter which begins; perhaps even Moscow may begin); we will win *absolutely* and *unquestionably*.

To Lenin, the consequences of the Kornilov Affair made his political strategy, first formulated in April, all the more alluring. It consisted of five simple promises to major sectors of Russian society. The Bolsheviks would quickly make peace with Germany, they would permit peasants to seize land, they would urge workers to seize factories, they would encourage soviets that had been established nationwide to assume the role of local governments, and they would permit the secession of ethnic minorities in the outlying regions. In fact, none of these promises was consistent with Bolshevik policies, and several deviated sharply from Marxist doctrine. After the Bolsheviks came to power, they, like their predecessors, wanted to prevent the dissolution of the Russian state. Hence, they tried to halt the disintegration of the army and opposed the claims to independence of most minorities. On the agrarian question, they were firmly opposed to dividing the countryside into smallholdings owned by peasants; they favored nationalization of the land. As committed Marxists, the Bolsheviks favored workers' control of individual factories; however, the goal was not control by workers at the local level but nationalization of industry with control in the hands of appointees of the national government. Finally, the Bolsheviks favored a centralized political regime in which major decisions were made and enforced by the political leadership in the capital, not by soviets on the local level. For Lenin, these were all matters to be handled once his party was in power; in the fall of 1917, his primary concern was to achieve it.

That turned out to be easier than anyone had imagined. Mass discontent with the existing regime became deeper and more widespread than ever before, in large part because Kerensky had completely failed to restore public confidence in his government. He also made several decisions that were bound to exacerbate public distrust of the authorities in Petrograd. He reshuffled his cabinet and appointed three Kadets to high positions, even though in the public mind the liberal party was widely believed to have been sympathetic to Kornilov. Moreover, Kerensky made only half-hearted attempts to initiate legal actions against the rebels, which troubled his supporters and raised further questions about the Prime Minister's complicity in the plot.

Preparing for revolution

On the other hand, the Bolsheviks were reinvigorated and full of confidence, although not all the party leaders were convinced that the time for a working class revolution had arrived. Lenin had remained in hiding in Finland ever since the upheaval in July, but couriers frequently brought messages to his colleagues in the capital, urging them to prepare for the toppling of the government. Trotsky was his leading supporter and spokesman in Petrograd. At the time of the March revolution, Trotsky had been in New York, where he earned his living from journalism and lecturing. He lived in an inexpensive apartment in the Bronx, but for him and his family it was luxurious: 'for the first time in his life,' Isaac Deutscher noted in his biography, 'the future leader of the revolution had a telephone in his home.' However, Trotsky quickly became restless and wanted to participate in the upheaval in his homeland. On 27 March, he and a few other émigrés boarded a Norwegian boat headed for Europe. Its first stop was Halifax, Nova Scotia, where British naval policemen forced all the Russian émigrés to disembark, before moving them to a camp for German prisoners of war in Amherst. The British government, unlike the German government, was eager to prevent a charismatic leader of the Left from reaching Petrograd, where he was bound to stir up the masses against the Provisional Government. Instead, Trotsky, a powerful orator with a gift for *bons mots*, did his best to arouse opposition to the war among the German prisoners. After German officers urged the commandant of the camp to prohibit Trotsky from addressing the prisoners, the Russian had to halt his effort to radicalize the Germans. In the meantime, Miliukov, then the Foreign Minister in the Provisional Government, was prevailed upon to protest Trotsky's detention. On 16 April, Trotsky was allowed to leave the camp and a few days later boarded a boat for Finland. From there he took a train to Petrograd, arriving on 4 May.

Trotsky was as passionate a revolutionary as Lenin, but they had their differences over doctrine and tactics. When the schism in Russian Social Democracy occurred in 1903, Trotsky sided with the Mensheviks and for well over a decade rejected Lenin's conception of a tightly organized socialist party dominated by a small group at the top. Lenin, on the other hand, was not taken with the doctrine of permanent revolution, which Trotsky had put forth in 1905. Soon after Trotsky arrived in Petrograd in 1917, he was appointed to the Executive of the Soviet, but he aligned himself with neither the Bolsheviks nor the Mensheviks. He belonged to the *Mezhrayonka* (Inter-Borough Organization), whose creation he had inspired while still abroad. This was a small group that maintained its independence, but from the beginning it felt more comfortable ideologically with the Bolsheviks than the Mensheviks. Shortly after Trotsky's arrival in Petrograd, the group joined the Leninists and Trotsky gave up his opposition to Lenin's views on party organization. As already noted, Lenin had concluded that Russia did not need to undergo a purely bourgeois revolution and could move directly to socialism. From that time, the two worked together closely and except for some differences over tactical issues, they collaborated in leading the second revolution and taking the first steps to introduce social-ism. Lenin was clearly the most powerful and celebrated leader, but Trotsky did not lag far behind.

Lenin, while still holed up in Vyborg, Finland, bombarded his colleagues in the capital with letters urging them to waste no time in leading the masses to a revolution for socialism. In a letter of 24 October to the Central Committee of the Bolshevik Party, he predicted that 'history will not forgive revolutionaries for procrastinating when they could be victorious today (will certainly be victorious today), while they risk losing much, in fact, everything, tomorrow.' It would be a 'disaster' to wait until the convocation of the entire Congress of the Soviets, scheduled to meet on 25 October, to vote on the question of overthrowing the government. The people, he insisted:

> … have the right and are in duty bound to decide such
> questions not by a vote, but by force in critical moments

of revolution; the people have the right and are in duty bound to direct their representatives, even their best representatives, and not to wait for them.

The government, he continued, was 'wavering' and it 'must be *destroyed* at all costs. To delay will be fatal.' Lenin knew that two members of the Bolshevik Central Committee, G. E. Zinoviev and L. B. Kamenev, opposed his strategy and he made clear that he had no use for them. He advised them to 'found their own party;' they would be supported by only a 'few dozen disoriented people or from candidates to the Constituent Assembly,' for which he had little use. Certainly, the 'workers will not join such a party.'

Trotsky assumed leadership of the Military Revolutionary Committee, created on 9 October to supervise the defense of Petrograd in the event that the Provisional Government left the city to evade the German troops that were poised to capture the city. However, the city remained in Russian hands, and very quickly the committee turned its attention to planning and organizing an uprising, and as its leader Trotsky became the guiding force of the insurrection. He frequently spoke at meetings of the soviet; he invariably advocated radical policies, but at the same time he did not want to let it be known that the Bolsheviks were planning an insurrection. When, during a session of the Petrograd Soviet, a deputy confronted the Bolsheviks and asked point blank whether they were preparing to seize power, Trotsky went to the podium and delivered an answer that has been described as a 'masterpiece of diplomatic camouflage.' He declared that the Bolsheviks were organizing a staff for the seizure of power but that no decision had been taken to unleash an insurrection. Such a decision would have to be taken by the Petrograd soviet. This answer was technically correct, but it was widely known that the Bolsheviks were making extensive preparations to seize power. Indeed, the Central Committee of the Bolshevik Party had already expressed support of such a move. Isaac Deutscher, Trotsky's biographer and defender, argued that he was under no obligation to reveal that decision because the Central Committee was a 'private body.'

The critical vote of the Central Committee had actually taken place on 10 October, under circumstances that would be amusing, were the decision not so momentous. A suitable place had to be found for the meeting, for Lenin, still in hiding, was to attend and had to take every precaution not to be seen by the police. Mrs. Sukhanov came to the rescue. Her sympathies lay with the Bolsheviks, but her husband, N. Sukhanov, was a left-wing Menshevik and journalist with a passion for attending as many deliberations of the soviet and other political groups as possible. His apartment in Karpovka was quite a distance— about five miles—from the Smolny, formerly a finishing school for girls of aristocratic families that had become the home of the Smolny Institute, where the soviet now met, and consequently he often spent nights somewhere near his office. On 10 October, his wife gave him 'a friendly, disinterested piece of advice—not to inconvenience myself by a further journey after work.' So the 'lofty assemblage had a complete guarantee against my arrival.' Sukhanov referred to the meeting as one of the 'novel jokes of the merry muse of History.'

Several members of the Central Committee arrived from Moscow and the 'Lord of Hosts,' as Sukhanov called Lenin, 'appeared in a wig, but without his beard. Zinoviev appeared with a beard, but without his shock of hair,' and thus both succeeded in evading the police. The meeting lasted some ten hours. In the end, the vote was ten to two in favor of placing the proposal to stage an uprising on the agenda of the Bolshevik Party, the two holdouts being Zinoviev and Kamenev.

The proposal to waste no time before launching the uprising on the evening of 24 October was based on an important consideration. Trotsky argued that it would be helpful to anticipate the meeting of the Congress of Soviets scheduled for 25 October. It seemed certain that the Bolsheviks would enjoy the support of a majority at the congress because a fair number of people on the non-Bolshevik Left would side with them. Hence, the congress could be asked to vote in favor of the uprising, giving the seizure of power the appearance of national support. Lenin at first rejected this plan on the ground that the congress's meeting was irrelevant. The critical point for him was to seize power, but a majority favored Trotsky's plan and in the end Lenin accepted it.

Kerensky's incompetence

The government did not know the details of the Bolshevik plans, but it knew as early as mid-October, as did many in the capital, that an attempt would soon be made to seize power. The Prime Minister was confident that he would be able to crush the Bolsheviks easily once they called on their supporters to move against the authorities. He boasted to his subordinates, and to foreign diplomats in Petrograd, that he had nothing to fear. On several occasions, he told British Ambassador George Buchanan that 'I only wish that [the Bolsheviks] would come out, and I will then put them down,' but he waited until 24 October before taking any action to nip the revolt in the bud. He shut down the Bolshevik newspaper *Rabochii Put*, which was exactly the provocation Trotsky had hoped for to justify attacking the government. On the same day, he gave the order to armed Bolsheviks to occupy key government buildings and called on Kerensky to surrender. The helplessness of the government became evident at once. Soldiers remained in the barracks and refused to come to the support of the authorities. Only a small battalion of women could be counted upon to defend the Winter Palace, where the government was meeting. Realizing the hopelessness of their situation, the ministers offered no resistance when armed

Bolsheviks appeared. Kerensky managed to escape by car, dressed as a woman, which enabled him to leave the capital. He visited various military installations in the hope of enlisting support, but was so discredited that his appeals were rejected.

The truth is that by late October, power lay in the streets of the capital and all the Bolsheviks had to do was pick it up. The conquest of power did not follow any one pattern. In Moscow, the Bolsheviks encountered more resistance than in the capital, but after some fierce fighting they prevailed. It did not take long for the Bolsheviks to take control of the rest of the country, at least the urban centers. There were remarkably few casualties in the capital, far fewer even than in February; it has been estimated that a few Red Guards were wounded, but apparently there were no fatalities. Early in 1918, Lenin himself acknowledged that taking power had been 'extremely easy.' The magnitude of the achievements of Lenin and Trotsky becomes all the more striking when it is realized that the Bolsheviks throughout Russia commanded a membership of only about 200,000 and the proletariat, in whose name the revolution was staged, numbered perhaps 3.5 million out of a total population of about 150 million.

Of course, on the day of the revolution neither Lenin nor Trotsky could have been certain of a quick and easy victory. They spent that evening in one of the rooms next to the large hall in the Smolny, where the Second Congress of the Soviets was scheduled to be held. Lenin was nervous and plied Trotsky with questions about the progress of the revolution. Trotsky, too, was restless, and neither could sleep. Hours later, when it was clear that the Bolsheviks had taken power, 'at least in Petrograd,' Lenin looked 'softly at [Trotsky], with that sort of awkward shyness that with him indicates intimacy.' "You know," he says hesitatingly, "from persecution and a life underground, to come so suddenly into power. ..." He pauses for the right word. "*Es schwindelt*" [It makes me dizzy], he concludes, changing suddenly to German, and circling his hand around his head. We look at each other and laugh a little.'

A day later, at a meeting of the Central Committee of the Bolshevik Party, Lenin put forward Trotsky's name for election as Chairman of the People's Commissars, the highest position in the new government. Trotsky 'sprang' to his feet and indicated that the nomination was 'unexpected' and 'inappropriate.' 'Why not?' Lenin asked. 'You were at the head of the Petrograd Soviet that seized power.' Trotsky would not hear of it because Lenin had been the strategist of the seizure of power and he had inspired the masses to follow the Bolsheviks. A few days later, Lenin said, 'There is not a better Bolshevik than Trotsky.'

Lenin then suggested that Trotsky be appointed Commissar of the Interior, in many ways the second most important post in the government, for its assignment would be to 'fight off the counterrevolution.' Again, Trotsky would not hear of it, but this time he offered a different objection: 'Was it worthwhile to put into our enemies' hands such an additional weapon as my Jewish origins?' Lenin was irritated by that argument: 'We are having a great international revolution,' he said. 'Of what importance are such trifles?' Trotsky agreed that a great revolution was in progress, yet 'there are still a good many fools left.' He prevailed but did accept the foreign affairs portfolio. With the onset of the Civil War, Trotsky was named Commissar of War. For over six years, until Lenin's death in 1924, he was the second most powerful man in the country. Lenin held the position of Chairman of the Council of People's Commissars, a title that made him head of the government.

Lenin's hunt for support

On 26 October 1917, when victory was assured, Lenin entered the hall where the Congress of Soviets held its meeting. The Bolsheviks enjoyed a majority, so it was not surprising that the delegates greeted their leader with thunderous applause. His first words evoked another 'overwhelming human roar: "We shall now proceed to construct the Socialist order."' He then listed the agenda of the new government:

> The first thing is the adoption of practical measures to realize peace ... We shall offer peace to the peoples of all the belligerent countries, peace upon the basis of the Soviet terms—no annexations, no indemnities, and the right of self-determination of peoples. At the same time, according to our promise, we shall publish and repudiate the secret treaties ... The question of War and Peace is so clear that I think that I may, without preamble, read the project of a Proclamation to the Peoples of All the Belligerent Countries.

After the Congress voted unanimously to support the proclamation on peace, Lenin proceeded to outline his domestic program.

In keeping with a promise he had made earlier in 1917, he vowed to enact the Socialist Revolutionary land program, which called for the distribution of all land to the peasants. As already noted, the SR platform deviated sharply from the standard Bolshevik program, which called for nationalization of all land. However, adopting it was one of Lenin's shrewdest moves, because it assured him of the support, or at least the political neutrality, of many peasants, still by far the largest social group in the country. Then, Lenin promised to introduce workers' control in all industrial, commercial, and agricultural enterprises, and to embark on the equalization of wages. All titles in the army, as well as the requirement to salute officers, would be abolished. Soldiers' committees would elect their officers. Finally, the marriage and divorce laws, which were archaic and kept women in subservience, would be swept aside. These measures amounted to a fundamental economic and social revolution, although it should be noted that only the last remained a permanent feature of the Soviet Union.

When it came to the new political order, the Bolsheviks were far less innovative. Despite pressure from other socialist parties for the creation of a coalition government, they stood their ground and in so doing expressed their contempt for other socialists, some of whom also considered themselves orthodox Marxists. The dispute came to a head during one of the early meetings of the Second Congress of the Soviets. Martov, a leader of the Mensheviks, introduced a motion calling for the formation of a coalition government representing all parties in the Soviet, that is, all the socialist parties. In his view, only in that way could an outburst of violence be prevented. When the Bolsheviks rejected his proposal, he made a serious mistake; he walked out, joining other socialists who had quit the proceedings in protest against the *coup*. It left the Bolsheviks in full control.

It also gave Trotsky an opportunity to demonstrate the Bolsheviks' determination to hold on to power and to heap scorn on their former colleagues. As Martov was leaving the hall, Trotsky assured the delegates that the departure of the Mensheviks would not sway the new rulers to change course. 'The rising of the popular masses,' he declared, 'needs no justification. What has taken place is an insurrection not a conspiracy. We have hardened the revolutionary energy of the workers and soldiers of Petrograd. We have openly steeled the will of the masses for a rising, not a conspiracy.' Then he unleashed a personal attack on the recently departed delegates:

No, a compromise is no good here. To those who have walked out and to those who come with such proposals [for a coalition government], we must say: 'You are pitiful isolated individuals, you are bankrupt; you have played out your role. Go where you belong: to the dustbin of history.'

In its harshness, Trotsky's dismissal of the Mensheviks gave a foretaste of the new rulers' mode of governing.

Shortly after their ascent to power, the Bolsheviks issued a decree suppressing newspapers critical of the new order, which amounted to a repudiation of a reform establishing freedom of the press that had been introduced by the Provisional Government. This measure was supposed to have been temporary, designed to shield the authorities at a time of crisis, but censorship of the press became a permanent feature of Communist rule.

On 7 December, before any indications of organized resistance to the new regime, the Bolshevik government established the *Cheka* (an abbreviation for All-Russian Extraordinary Commission to Combat Counter-Revolution and Sabotage), the secret police charged with rooting out opposition to the new government. Its Director, F. E. Dzerzhinsky, made no effort to disguise the function of his organization: 'We represent,' he declared, 'organized terror—this must be said clearly.' He cast his net wide in arresting citizens suspected of opposition, a policy consistent with Lenin's view that no mercy should be shown to such people. In an article entitled 'How to Organize Competition,' written early in January 1918 and published in *Pravda* on 20 January 1929, Lenin called for a variety of methods to achieve:

... the common aim—to clean the land of Russia of all sorts of vermin, of fleas, of bedbugs—the rich, and so on and so forth. In one place half a score of rich, a dozen crooks, half a dozen workers who shirk their work ... will be put in prison. In another place they will be put to cleaning latrines. In a third place they will be provided with 'yellow tickets' after they have served their time, so that all the people shall have them under surveillance, as harmful persons, until they reform. In a fourth place, one out of every ten idlers will be shot on the spot. In a fifth place mixed methods may be adopted ... The more variety there will be, the better and richer will be our general experience, the more certain and rapid will be the success of socialism.

He warned that 'weakness, hesitation or sentimentality ... would be a great crime to Socialism.'

Although the Cheka immediately sought to crush the opposition to Bolshevism—it executed some 882 people within the first six months of its existence—it did not initiate a systematic crackdown until the summer of 1918, when two events triggered what came to be known as the 'Red Terror.' On 30 August 1918, Moisei Uritsky, the People's Commissar for Internal Affairs and the head of the Cheka in Petrograd, was assassinated by a young officer, but a far more dramatic murder was attempted on the same day in Moscow. Fanya Kaplan fired three shots at Lenin as he emerged from the Mikhelson Factory, where he had given a speech to workers. One bullet struck Lenin in the arm and did not seriously injure him, but another pierced his neck, causing considerable bleeding. He fell down and was whisked off unconscious to the Kremlin, where several doctors treated him. Initially, the doctors feared for his life, but he made a rapid recovery and resumed full-time work in his office by the end of October.

Although the assassination and attempted assassination had not been coordinated, both were politically motivated. Kaplan was known to be a terrorist as far back as 1906, when she was only sixteen. At that time, she identified herself as an anarchist and was arrested because a bomb she was preparing to use against the Governor-General of Kiev exploded prematurely. She was sentenced to a lifelong term of hard labor in Siberia. Released after the first revolution in 1917, she joined an offshoot of the Socialist Revolutionary Party, which had always taken a benign view of terrorism. Kaplan was incensed with Lenin because he had dismissed the Constituent Assembly. Despite her vow not to leave the scene of the crime, she ran away, but was quickly caught by the police, and after repeated refusals to cooperate with her interrogators, was executed on 13 September.

What followed, in the words of William Henry Chamberlin, who wrote the first scholarly and comprehensive history of the Russian Revolution, was 'one of the most ferocious outbursts of organized revolutionary terrorism since the French Revolution.' The number of people, nearly all well-to-do, executed by the Cheka over a two-year period remains in dispute: some claim that it was about 12,350. Chamberlin's estimate was 50,000, and the most recent scholarly work on the subject (by G. Leggett) concluded that the total killed during the Red Terror ran to about 140,000. Certainly, the rapid increase in the size of the secret police would suggest that its activities increased exponentially. In May 1919, the Cheka's 'internal army' numbered about 120,000; a year later, it had increased to 240,000.

Peace with Germany

Lenin understood all along that repression and economic concessions alone would not suffice to consolidate his regime. It was vital to end the war, which continued to drain Russia's resources and became ever more unpopular. Reaching agreement with the Germans proved far more difficult than Lenin had anticipated. On 20 November, a committee headed by A. A. Joffe, formerly a Menshevik and a friend of Trotsky, met with a German delegation in the Polish city of Brest-Litovsk, the seat of the German headquarters. Within three days, the parties agreed to a ceasefire, but the far more difficult task was to negotiate a permanent end to the war.

On 27 December, the negotiations resumed; this time, Trotsky headed the Russian delegation, a sign of the importance the Bolsheviks attached to a settlement. It turned out that his appointment may not have been wise. As soon as he arrived in

Brest-Litovsk, he and members of his entourage passed leaf-
lets to German soldiers, urging them to prepare for a socialist
revolution. The stodgy German diplomats and generals were not
amused, but worse was to come for the Russians. The Germans
offered a peace plan that provided for the separation of Poland
from Russia and for the annexation by Germany of territory in
western Russia, which would mean loss of the Ukraine, Lithuania, and southern Latvia. Trotsky immediately declared that he
would have to return to Petrograd for consultations.

Lenin favored acceptance of the German terms because he
believed that Russia needed a 'breathing spell' so that Bolshevik power could be consolidated. However, a group within
the leadership, headed by N. I. Bukharin, who believed that
the revolution would spread to Europe, urged rejection of the
terms and resumption of the war, primarily by partisan actions,
against the German army, which continued to advance into
Russia. He also called for intense agitation in Central Europe in
favor of revolution, which, he contended, would so frighten the
German government that it would reevaluate its position regarding a peace settlement with Russia. Trotsky came up with an
altogether baffling response to the German peace terms. Russia
should adopt the following policy: 'Neither war nor peace.' In
other words, Russia would no longer wage war and would not
sign a peace settlement. Out of sixty-three votes at a meeting
of party leaders, Lenin's proposal garnered only fifteen. He also
lost in the Central Committee, although by a very small margin.
When Trotsky informed the Germans that their terms were
unacceptable, the generals responded by ordering a new offensive and penetrated further into Russia. Trotsky now changed his
mind and Lenin's motion to accept Germany's peace offer passed
in the Central Committee by a vote of seven to six.

The losses incurred by Russia as a result of the peace settlement known as the Treaty of Brest-Litovsk (signed on 3 March,
1918) were enormous: 26 percent of its population, 27 percent

of its arable land, 32 percent of its average yearly crops, 26 percent of its railway system, 33 percent of its manufacturing industries, 73 percent of its iron industries, and 75 percent of its coal mines. Russia's economy declined sharply, which is exactly what the enemy leaders wanted, because it made the country dependent on Germany. It would also provide Germany with much-needed agricultural goods. Lenin's calculation was quite different: he was certain that the socialist revolution would soon break out in Germany, and once that had occurred, the Treaty of Brest-Litovsk would be null and void. His calculation that Russia would recover the lands it had lost proved to be right, but not for the reasons he gave.

The Bolsheviks' expectation of world revolution turned out to be their greatest misjudgment. They looked upon Germany as most likely to be the first to follow their example. The country was highly industrialized, its working class was sophisticated, its socialist party the largest in the world, and several of its social-ist theorists ranked among the world's most insightful exponents of Marx's teachings. These considerations led the Bolsheviks to endless misinterpretations of developments in Germany. On 21 November 1917, *Izvestiia*, a Bolshevik newspaper, assured its readers that the 'German proletariat is already mobilizing its forces and ... the struggle has begun, even though it has not yet assumed a violent character.' Other articles early in Febru-ary 1918 announced that soviets had been created and that the people of Berlin were arming themselves in preparation for the 'struggle for a class dictatorship of the proletariat.' By March 1919, Lenin even believed that a socialist revolution might well break out in the United States in the not-too-distant future. He found it 'extremely interesting' that soviets were gaining popu-larity in America and predicted that 'sooner or later they will take power into their own hands.' He based this fanciful forecast on information he had received about the creation of a General Strike Committee that had led a five-day general strike in Seattle in February 1919, which in fact did not have the kind of political significance Lenin attached to it.

Apparently, the Russian revolutionaries did not understand that during the forty-two years of its existence the German Social Democratic Party had shifted away from radicalism and that the German working class generally approved of the abandonment of the far Left. Nor did they understand the significance of the criticism leveled at Leninism by western Marxists who rejected the undemocratic features of Bolshevism. Most notably, Karl Kautsky, the movement's foremost theorist, published a short book in 1918 attacking the October revolution as a distortion of Marxism; by then, he and Lenin were not on speaking terms. Moreover, the German Social Democratic Party made it abundantly clear that it would not follow Russia's path to socialism. Eventually, the failure of any Western country to follow Russia's example deeply influenced developments in Russia; in the 1920s the leaders focused on 'socialism in one country,' a turn that led them to build a socialist order at home regardless of developments in the rest of the world.

Death knell for democracy

In January 1918, the Bolsheviks took a step that confirmed the worst fears of democratic socialists. They dispersed the Constituent Assembly, which had finally met after several postponements of its election. The Assembly had been the great hope of those who had taken over the reins of government after the first revolution in March 1917. For the first time in Russia's history, an assembly elected by all adult citizens, including women, was to write a constitution for the country that would establish a truly democratic system of rule. In the months after the collapse of the autocracy, even the Bolsheviks supported the election and convocation of the Assembly. It is understandable that under the chaotic circumstances of 1917 it took time to organize and hold elections, but it was unfortunate for those who believed in democracy that the process was not completed sooner. The Assembly was the one institution that might have induced sufficient calm to make possible the formation of a government that could have put the country on an even keel. Thirty-six million citizens, over 48 percent of the eligible voters, cast ballots, and the Bolsheviks received a mere one-fourth. Of the 707 deputies, 175 were Bolsheviks, 370 were Socialist Revolutionaries of the Right, and 40 were Socialist Revolutionaries of the Left. Seventeen Kadets and eighteen Mensheviks were also elected. The remaining 120 seats were distributed among other small parties.

Even before the Assembly met, Lenin questioned the legitimacy of the elections and, more important, the legitimacy of the Assembly as a body speaking for the people. He pointed out that the Socialist Revolutionaries had entered the elections as a single party, but since that time—on 28 November—a sector of the party, the Left Socialist Revolutionaries, had come out in support of the Bolshevik seizure of power and had in fact joined a new coalition government. Lenin claimed that if the change of heart by a substantial sector of the SR Party had been generally known at the time of the elections, the pro-Bolshevik movements would have won a majority. On 25 December, eleven days before the Assembly met, Lenin published his 'Theses on the Constituent Assembly,' in which he made clear that he put no stock in that body regardless of the timing of the split within the Socialist Revolutionary Party. 'A republic of soviets,' he declared, 'is a higher form than the customary bourgeois republic with its constituent assembly.' Consequently, the Assembly must accept 'Soviet power [and] the Soviet revolution.' Otherwise 'a crisis in connection with the Constituent Assembly can be solved only by revolutionary means.'

The Assembly met as scheduled in the afternoon of 18 January, but under circumstances that could leave no one in doubt that it would accomplish nothing. A peaceful demonstration of about fifty thousand supporters was quickly and harshly dispersed by armed men under the control of the Bolsheviks. As the delegates approached the Tauride Palace, where the meetings were to be held, they noticed—as reported by V. M. Zenzinov—that the entire square in front of it was:

> ... filled with artillery, machine guns, field kitchens. Machine gun cartridge belts were piled up pell-mell ... Everywhere there were armed men, mostly sailors and Latvians ... The number of armed men and weapons, the sound of clanking, created the impression of an encampment getting ready either to defend itself or to attack.

Zenzinov also recalled that many delegates walked into the palace determined to work on a democratic constitution, but they feared that they 'would not return home alive.' The Socialist Revolutionaries, who had a majority of the delegates, elected their leader, Victor Chernov, to be President of the Assembly, and he immediately faced a move by the Bolsheviks designed to make it impossible for the delegates to accomplish their appointed task. F. F. Raskolnikov, a Bolshevik naval officer from Kronstadt, introduced a motion calling on the Assembly to renounce its assigned task and to devote itself to reorganizing 'society on a socialist basis.' When this motion was defeated by a vote of 237 to 136, all the Bolsheviks walked out. The remaining delegates continued to listen to speeches until 4 a.m., at which time a 'Citizen Sailor' approached the chairman and asked that the meeting be ended because 'the guard is tired.' Chernov objected and asked who had given the order to adjourn, but when armed soldiers marched in to supplement those already in the hall, the chairman, after allowing discussion to continue for twenty more minutes, halted the proceedings until 5 p.m. But in the meantime, the Bolsheviks had decided to dissolve the Assembly, and the delegates were never reassembled.

Some historians have argued that the dissolution of the Constituent Assembly marked the end of the revolution because the Bolsheviks had now shown that they had no intention of giving up power. E. H. Carr, the noted English historian, made a similar point when he referred to Lenin's vow to disperse the Assembly as 'a final tearing asunder of the veil of bourgeois constitutionalism.' The dispersion of the elected delegates charged with writing a democratic constitution for Russia was doubtless an important event, but it is not clear that it should be considered the end of the upheaval of 1917. It merely indicated that Lenin would not easily cede power and that he was not committed to democratic rule, which had been known at least since 1902, when he published *What Is to Be Done?* In January 1918, several of his most important goals had not yet been achieved and one may doubt whether he himself believed that the revolution had ended. Russia had not yet extricated itself from the war, the economy was in rapid decline, disposition of the lands owned by landlords and the state had not been completed, and clear rules on the management of factories seized from private owners had not yet been formulated. In other words, while the people who ran the country were socialists, socialism remained to be established. It would take years for anything resembling the socialist ideal to be realized, and when it was, the social and economic order in Russia looked quite different from the aspirations and promises of Lenin and other Marxists in the years before 1917.

6

The struggle to retain power

Within months of seizing power, the Bolsheviks, who in March 1918 adopted the more easily recognizable name 'Communists,' faced challenges so severe that it was by no means certain that they would be able to cope with them. In the first place, the economy had disintegrated. Because peasants were unwilling to sell the grain they harvested at the prevailing low prices, the essential staple of most households was in short supply. At the same time, industrial production had declined at an alarming rate: in 1917, industrial output amounted to a mere 33.8 percent of the total in 1913. As a consequence, there simply were not enough manufactured goods to give farmers a return on their crops, a further disincentive to maximize their yields. The danger of mass starvation loomed in the cities, exacerbated by the deterioration of trains and other means of transportation, which prevented satisfactory exchanges between the countryside and the cities.

Politically, too, the authorities faced unsettling and unexpected challenges. In elections to local soviets in May and June 1918, the Mensheviks won numerous victories; it looked as though sentiment among the working class was turning sharply against the new rulers. In June 1918, the government made a bold move to deal with the crumbling economy by introducing a radical program known as 'War Communism.' The authorities declared all grain to be a government monopoly and called on poor peasants in the villages to form committees to enforce the requisition of grain from well-to-do peasants; as a reward, committee members would be given a share of the grain, as well as a portion of the industrial goods that reached the villages. These policies were not designed just to deal with the economic crisis. They also served an ideological purpose: they brought 'class war' into the villages.

In November 1918, the government took an additional step toward socialism by nationalizing all trade. It called for the establishment of a network of cooperative stores to distribute goods, which were strictly rationed. This measure quickly led to the virtual elimination of private trading. Money, credit, and prices no longer played a significant role in the national economy.

The banks had been nationalized soon after the Bolshevik seizure of power, and the only way for the government to obtain currency was to resort to the printing press, a practice that led to severe inflation. As money declined in value, the government began to collect taxes by forcing citizens to make their payments in kind. Soon wages in many establishments were also paid in kind. By the second half of 1918, 27.9 percent of all wages were paid with goods; by 1921, that had risen to 94 percent. Russia, it was said, had reverted to a medieval economy, in which barter was the principal mode of exchanging goods.

Industrial productivity remained abysmal, in part because of a measure introduced by the Bolsheviks in November 1917. The government, in keeping with its ideological convictions, imposed workers' control in all factories, a measure that undermined efficiency, since workers had little experience in deciding how to produce high-quality goods at reasonable cost. Lenin realized this; early in 1918 he restored one-man management and also brought back to their previous jobs specialists who had worked in factories before the revolution. In December 1918, the authorities in Moscow, in an effort to increase production, issued a decree compelling all citizens between the ages of sixteen and fifty to hold down a job. No one could move from one job to another without permission from a state agency formed to supervise what came to be known as the 'nationalization of labor.' This measure, too, did little to improve efficiency in industry. The government then adopted the practice of drawing up national plans on the assumption that productivity could be stimulated by setting specific targets for industries and factories, but conditions were so chaotic and hardships so severe that decisions made by central agencies in Moscow could not be implemented.

By 1920, it was clear that far from solving the country's economic problems, War Communism had led to a further decline that can only be described as catastrophic. In the country-side, peasants produced less because they did not wish to surrender their crops to the committees of the poor. During a period of eight years, from 1913 to 1921, agricultural production declined by 54 percent. Malnutrition was widespread; more than seven million people died from starvation or disease, most notably from the epidemic known as the Spanish flu, which also affected other countries. It has been estimated that in the three years from 1918 to 1920 the death rate more than doubled. Large cities saw their populations decline dramatically, as workers returned to farms to feed their families. Moscow lost about one half its population and Petrograd lost even more. Both cities were major industrial centers, and as a result of the exodus the number of workers declined by one half from 1917 to 1920.

The Bolsheviks could claim certain positive results, mainly ideological, from the stringent economic policies imposed under War Communism. The government gained control over the so-called commanding heights of the economy: large industries, transportation, banks, and foreign trade. In addition, some officials gained experience in administering certain important branches of industry, but the price the country paid for these benefits was high, leaving a large percentage of the population in dire straits.

Economic privation and loss in working class support were not the only challenges the Communists faced during their first years in power. They also confronted a military threat from a counterrevolution organized by the opposition to their rule, and from a band of invading armies composed of soldiers from fourteen countries. Some of the invaders intended to restore the eastern front against Germany, others were determined to crush Bolshevism, and some wished to grab land from a weakened Russia, while the primary aim of the United States in sending troops into Russia was to prevent Japan from seizing a huge swath of land in the Transbaikal Region and further east. Lenin turned to Trotsky, his most dynamic and capable subordinate, to build a Red Army to defend the revolution. Trotsky's success in this endeavor probably marks his greatest achievement.

He knew that a major reason for the collapse of the Provisional Government had been its inability to maintain discipline in the army, and he therefore concentrated on creating a military force that would carry out the orders of the new government. 'An army cannot be built without repression,' he wrote in his autobiography:

> Masses of men cannot be led to death unless the army command has the death-penalty in its arsenal. So long as those malicious tailless apes that are so proud of their technical achievements—the animals we call men—will build armies and wage wars, the command will always be obliged to place the soldiers between the possible death in the front and the inevitable one in the rear.

True, Kerensky and Kornilov had applied this principle and the army had still crumbled. That did not happen to the Red Army, Trotsky later explained, because the 'strongest cement in the new army was the ideas of the October revolution.'

Trotsky proceeded systematically in creating the Red Army. First, he ordered compulsory military training for all workers and peasants who did not hire labor—this provision was to assure that no one hostile to Communism would serve in the new army. To maintain discipline, he restored the death penalty for violators of military rules. Deserters, who were numerous, were occasionally shot or forced to serve in 'punishment units.' When an entire unit failed to carry out orders and fled from the enemy, one in ten was to be shot on the spot. Trotsky also ended the election of officers by ordinary soldiers, a reform introduced only a few months earlier; it had quickly become evident that it had not enhanced either efficiency or bravery at the front. When officers who had served in the tsarist army volunteered to join the revolutionary forces, Trotsky welcomed them but warned that if they deserted, their families would be punished. To keep an eye on officers and to conduct propaganda among the troops, politically trustworthy commissars were stationed throughout the army. Within a few months, the Red Army developed into a reasonably effective fighting force. There is a noteworthy irony in this. Only fifteen months earlier, the far left, including the Bolsheviks, had campaigned for the abolition of the death penalty, a stand that was important in securing a majority for the Bolsheviks in the Petrograd Soviet.

Civil war

The Civil War began in the spring of 1918, lasted for roughly three years, and cost the country about 800,000 lives. It was an extremely complicated struggle, as will be evident from a brief discussion of its main features. There were so many zigzags in the fighting that at times it was not clear which side had the upper hand. The counterrevolutionaries, soon to be known as the Whites (a throwback to the monarchists in France, whose standard was white), could count on the support of several groups whose ultimate goals were not identical. In the first place, a fair number of non-Bolshevik politicians who had been active in a wide range of political parties—including a few from the Socialist Revolutionary Party—supported the attempt to unseat the Communists. The Mensheviks remained aloof from this camp; a majority opposed the Leninists, but they refused to align themselves with the Whites, whom they regarded as reactionary. On the other hand, a sizable number of former officials in the Provisional Government joined the Whites, as did several nationalist groups seeking independence, as well as Cossacks and a fair number of intellectuals. The nationalists were especially powerful in the Ukraine, where the *Rada* (Supreme Council) proclaimed the Ukraine an independent People's Republic eleven days after the Bolshevik seizure of power. However, it was the senior officers of the Imperial army who composed what has been called the 'moving spirit' behind the effort to overthrow the new government.

The first skirmishes between foreign and Russian troops involved Czechs, not the armies of Western countries. A considerable number of Czech soldiers had been dispatched to the Eastern Front in 1914 by the Austro-Hungarian government, but they showed no interest in fighting against Russia, and many deserted to the Russian side. Thomas G. Masaryk, the leader of the Czech national movement, advised the deserters to form a special brigade, which by 1917 numbered about forty-five thousand men, and to join the fight against the Central Powers. Masaryk calculated that if the Czechs contributed to a victory by France, Great Britain, and the United States, he would have a voice at the peace conference and would be in a position to secure Czech independence from Austria-Hungary. The brigade had survived the collapse of the Eastern Front; Masaryk wanted to send the Czech soldiers to France to continue fighting, in hopes of further enhancing the Czechs' bargaining power at the peace table. The Russians agreed to permit the Czechs to go to France by way of Vladivostok, the country's largest port on the Pacific Ocean, but only on condition that the troops would travel as 'free citizens,' with a minimum of arms. The Czechs refused to surrender their weapons. In what turned out to be a major blunder, Trotsky ordered Russian troops to disarm the Czechs, by force if necessary. A series of clashes broke out in Cheliabinsk in the Urals, which quickly spread all along the Trans-Siberian Railway. By 8 June 1918, the Czechs had taken control of several towns in the area, from Penza in south-central Russia, to Samara on the Volga, and Tomsk in Siberia.

The French government saw in this development an opportunity to realize its overall goal in Russia, and therefore urged the Czechs to stay put and become part of the foreign intervention. French troops had arrived in Murmansk in March 1918, and were followed in short order by additional forces in Archangel and Vladivostok. The successful action of the Czechs in seizing control of a sizable amount of Russian territory persuaded the French that it would be possible to overthrow the Communist government without massive intervention by Western troops. This assessment soon turned out to be a misapprehension of the military situation in Russia.

To help the Czechs and exploit the weakness of the Bolshevik government, in the summer of 1918 the British landed small numbers of troops on the coasts of the White and Black Seas. In addition, the Japanese, eager to extend their influence in Russia, landed troops on the coastal areas of the Sea of Japan. To check the advance of the Japanese, the United States sent a force of some thirteen thousand to Siberia and Archangel. Eventually, eleven other countries sent relatively small detachments of soldiers to Russia. All in all, by late 1918 over two hundred thousand foreign troops had invaded Russian soil. Although the foreign intervention was certainly unwelcome, it was never large enough or sufficiently coordinated enough to pose a serious threat to the regime. Also, public opinion in the interventionist Western countries opposed involvement in yet another military conflict so strongly that by 1921 nearly all the foreign troops were withdrawn.

The indigenous military opposition turned out to be a greater threat to the Communists, but divisions within that camp greatly weakened it. For one thing, the Whites consisted of members of five different groups, whose political programs differed sharply: the tsarists favored a return to the old order, the Octobrists called for a limited monarchy, the Kadets advocated Western-style democracy, the Socialist Revolutionaries wanted a democracy committed to the distribution of land to the peasants, and finally, the representatives of various national minorities pressed for autonomy and, in some cases, independence. The controversies were intense and prevented them from forming a solidly united front against the government. The only common denominator was a strong distaste for Communism.

Not only were the Communists a relatively united force, commanded by a strong leader, they also benefited from their control of central Russia, which enabled them to maintain close supervision of their forces. By contrast, the Whites operated on the periphery, where transportation was primitive, facilities for the production of weapons were scant, and communication between the various commanders was difficult. Moreover, no White commander was as skillful as Trotsky in creating an effective fighting force.

General A.V. Denikin was in some respects the most successful military leader of the Whites. A forty-six-year-old tsarist officer, Denikin had a distinguished military record. During World War I, he quickly rose through the ranks, and by the spring of 1917 was Chief of Staff to the Supreme Commander. He supported General Kornilov in his conflict with Kerensky; when Kornilov's movement collapsed, both were arrested. In December 1917, the two generals escaped from prison and devoted themselves to forming the Volunteer Army (or White Army) in south Russia. After a shell fired by Soviet troops killed Kornilov in April 1918, Denikin assumed the position of leader of the White Army in south Russia, although technically he remained subordinate to

Admiral A. V. Kolchak, who commanded the White Army in Siberia. Denikin built an armed force numbering slightly over 150,000 men; at the height of his power he ruled a vast area, with a population of about forty million. Although the course of the Civil War was incredibly complicated, a consideration of Denikin's successes and ultimate failure in south Russia sheds light on the fate of all the White armies, despite the significant differences in their experiences.

Militarily, Denikin scored some impressive victories and came close to toppling the Bolsheviks. In July 1919, his troops began to push toward the east and captured the important cities of Kursk, Voronezh, Chernigov, and Orel. The Whites were then some 250 miles from Moscow; by mid-October 1919, there seemed few additional obstacles in their march to the Communist capital. The only city that stood in their path was Tula. However, Denikin now faced a series of unexpected hurdles.

The first hurdle was military: the general ran out of badly needed reserves, because his exhausted army had been depleted by the dispatch of troops to the rear to subdue the roaming bands loyal to N. I. Makhno, the leader of the Free Territorial Society, which was hostile to any form of state authority, Communist or capitalist. Makhno resorted to guerrilla warfare to achieve his anarchist utopia, and by all accounts was not squeamish about the methods he used against anyone who stood in his way. He came to be known as the 'instigator' of 'military ravages' against innocent citizens and as a 'human monster' who reveled in the shedding of human blood. Makhno's attacks on innocent people were so widespread that Denikin had no choice but to assign part of his army to contain the anarchist.

In addition, Denikin faced a series of social and political tensions in the vast area under his control that he could not deal with, and this failure, as much as anything else, led to his undoing. To govern an area including numerous minorities and social groups, with conflicting interests and aspirations, requires political skills of a high order, but Denikin was politically naïve and inept. In some respects, he seemed to be enlightened and moderate; he always insisted that he was not a reactionary, and refused to approve the use of 'monarchist slogans' by the officers under his command. He frequently mentioned that he came from a 'humble background,' that his father had been a serf and had never risen beyond the level of a minor official. He had achieved his success in the military by dint of hard work and had none of the advantages of upper-class men who had acquired high positions through family influence. However, he did not support political liberalism; his deepest political conviction was nationalism. He summed up his most cherished ideal thus: 'Russia shall be great, united, undivided.' To most Russian peasants and workers in 1919, who were barely making ends meet, these words were not inspiring.

Denikin's nationalism was so fervent that he could not maintain good relations with the Ukrainian, Cossack, or Caucasian peoples in the region he governed, and their support was essential to winning the war against the Communists. He was remarkably unsophisticated in not perceiving that he had to adopt policies supported by his constituents. He often spoke of his open-mindedness, but did little to introduce badly needed reforms or to uphold those already introduced. Often his most ardent supporters took measures that seriously harmed the interests of ordinary peasants. In areas recaptured by Whites, and under his control, former landlords would return and reclaim land that had been seized by peasants, or given to them by the Bolsheviks. Nor was Denikin an effective leader. He could not maintain discipline within his ranks, or stop the pillaging that often took the form of anti-Jewish pogroms. In his autobiography, Denikin acknowledged his army's misconduct:

> The troops of the army of the south did not avoid
> the general malady and they blotted their reputation

by pogroms of Jews … The inner sores festered in the atmosphere of hatred … The pogroms brought suffering to the Jewish people, but they also affected the spirit of the troops, warped their minds and destroyed discipline.

Other White generals also noted the deleterious impact of the soldiers' rampages on the combat effectiveness of the entire army.

By the end of 1919, the Communists had inflicted one defeat after another on the Whites. In the fall of that year, the Whites were beaten back by the Reds near Petrograd, and then suffered another crushing defeat at the hands of General S. M. Budenny's troops near Voronezh, effectively ending the threat to Moscow. The tide had now definitively turned in favor of the Red Army.

Admiral Kolchak, who commanded the Whites in Siberia, fared even worse. Early in 1920, after being thoroughly defeated by government troops, he abdicated, leaving Denikin as the Supreme Commander. Kolchak placed himself at the mercy of the French and Czechs, who handed him over to the local radicals in Irkutsk. In short order, they shot him, even though Lenin professed not to have favored the execution, probably because he did not want to anger the Whites and thus encourage them to fight harder.

Even now, the revolution was not out of danger. In May 1920, Marshal J. K. Pilsudski, who had assumed leadership of the nationalist movement in Poland and played a leading role in regaining the country's independence in 1918, marched into Kiev with the intention of realizing a lifelong dream: to weaken Russia by establishing independence along its border of Finland, Latvia, Estonia, Lithuania, and the Ukraine. The conflict assumed the character of a seesaw. The Poles were defeated by the Russians, who then marched to the outskirts of Warsaw, only to be defeated by the Poles. Exhausted, the two sides agreed to a ceasefire in October 1920 and a peace treaty in March 1921, which gave Poland control of the western area of the Ukraine and parts of Belorussia.

At this point, only General P.N. Wrangel, who commanded an army of Whites in the Crimea, remained a potential threat to the Communists. As soon as the Leninists had made peace with Poland, they concentrated their forces in the Crimea and defeated Wrangel's army. Some small armies in various parts of Russia still offered armed resistance; they were defeated in the spring of 1921. The three years of war had been exhausting, but in the end the Communists were masters of a country similar in size to that of the Russian Empire, with the following exceptions: Finland, Estonia, Latvia, Lithuania, and Poland became independent states; Bessarabia became part of Romania; and parts of Belorussia and the Ukraine were annexed by Poland. A 'Far Eastern Republic' remained under Japanese occupation and some pockets of resistance to Soviet rule persisted in Central Asia for about another decade.

The early years of Soviet rule

Once the new boundaries of Russia had been set, Lenin and Trotsky turned their full attention to domestic political, and economic issues. The Communist Party ran the country, even though it had never received majority support in a free national election. Notably, however, in the early years of Soviet rule, the party itself was not run dictatorially. Its decisions were reached at the highest levels after long discussions and votes. For example, the Central Committee deliberated for some time on the Treaty of Brest-Litovsk before passing it by the narrowest of margins. Interestingly, the Left Socialist Revolutionaries, who had joined the government in December 1917, abandoned it six months later. They wanted to resume the war against Germany, but Lenin insisted on a breathing spell to enable the Communists to consolidate their power.

The leading organs of the Communist Party continued to discuss policy options on such matters as the control of industry the appropriateness of employing specialists who did not belong to the party, and the relations of the authorities with cooperatives and trade unions. The government adopted a relatively flexible position on these issues, but maintained a hard line toward political parties that refused to recognize the legitimacy of the new regime. In December 1917, non-socialist parties were outlawed. The Socialist Revolutionaries (SRs) were not affected by this decree, but when the SRs took positions that clearly challenged the legitimacy of Bolshevik rule, they, too, began to feel the wrath of the authorities.

Actually, the SRs adopted a program that placed them in an ambiguous position. They supported certain groups of Whites in their campaign to overthrow the Communists, but, at the same time, disavowed any support for reactionaries. They favored the distribution of all land to the peasants and, like some of their colleagues on the left, opposed the peace treaty with Germany. Relations between the SRs and the Bolsheviks were never exactly friendly, but after certain events in 1918 they became decidedly frosty. On 6 July, a SR shot and killed Count Wilhelm von Mirbach, the German ambassador to the Soviet Union; at the same time, the SRs staged uprisings in Moscow and Yaroslavl, both of which failed only after considerable blood had been shed. The Left SRs, who supported the Bolsheviks at the time of the Bolshevik seizure of power, were banned from membership in the soviets, and as the historian Evan Mawdsley put it, 'at this point the Soviet Union became a "one-party state." The hostility between the SRs and the Communists sharpened immensely in 1922, when several SR leaders were charged with organizing an attempt to assassinate Lenin, sponsoring other terrorist acts, and with having collaborated with General Denikin. At the trial, the defense was not allowed to question witnesses or to produce documents disproving the charges, rendering a verdict of guilty inevitable. Some of the accused received death sentences, which were eventually suspended, apparently because of extensive criticism of this harsh punishment. The accused were then given long prison sentences.

The government's policy toward the Mensheviks was rather complicated. They were Marxists, they had worked closely with Lenin and Trotsky for several years, and they did not call for the violent overthrow of the regime. Although they disapproved of the Communist government, they sought to replace it by constitutional means, and in that, were unique. They proposed reconvening the Constituent Assembly and called for freely elected soviets. Late in 1917, public support for the Mensheviks declined, because people on the Left were inclined to give the Bolsheviks the benefit of the doubt, but in 1918, as economic conditions worsened, the Mensheviks made a comeback and scored successes in elections to several local soviets. Contrary to all evidence, the government claimed that the Mensheviks were stirring up violent opposition and late in 1918, it closed down their press. At the same time, on 30 November, it legalized the Mensheviks as a political party, probably because it hoped that most of them would see the light and offer support to the new regime. Quite a few did precisely that.

The remaining Mensheviks continued to press for free elections and an end to persecution of the opposition. In addition, the Mensheviks called for the abandonment of War Communism and the adoption of economic policies that would introduce a limited free market. Their influence in the trade unions grew and it has been estimated that, together with other anti-Communist groups, they enjoyed a majority within the labor movement by 1921. This put Lenin in an awkward position. He was prepared to introduce major economic reforms along the lines proposed by the Mensheviks, but he did not want them to receive credit for the switch. He therefore ordered a massive crackdown. Although the government never officially outlawed the party, in the first three months of 1921 the police arrested three thousand Mensheviks; within a year, the movement ceased to be a viable party.

Lenin also faced considerable opposition within the ranks of his own party. The Left Communists, led by Bukharin, opposed the peace treaty with Germany and favored more radical economic policies, such as broader nationalization of industry and an increase in workers' power to control factories. In March 1919, a so-called Military Opposition emerged and demanded, among other things, that local Communist Party organizations be given a greater say in army affairs. Early in 1921, several party members formed the Workers Opposition, which called for free elections in trade unions and proposed that the unions be authorized to administer all industrial establishments. Its program was clearly designed to weaken the power of the Central Committee of the party, and when Alexandra Kollontai, who had achieved a degree of fame as the foremost female Bolshevik and as the People's Commissar of Social Welfare, joined this group, it acquired a leader who could attract wide attention to its demands.

A turn to the right: the new economic policy

Before Lenin could deal with the various disputes within the Communist Party, he was confronted with yet another surge of discontent that required immediate attention. In February 1921, workers in Petrograd launched a series of strikes to protest at food shortages. The Mensheviks took advantage of the unrest and began to agitate for democracy, at least for workers. The government quickly arranged for the shipment of substantial quantities of food to the capital and sanctioned the formation of 'food-finding expeditions by workers.' To prevent the spread of the strike, the police arrested many Mensheviks and Socialist Revolutionaries who had encouraged workers to join the protest movement.

News of the unrest had spread, and it served to spark far more serious disturbances in Kronstadt, a major military seaport seventeen miles west of Petrograd. The sailors in that city had long been considered model revolutionaries; in 1917, Trotsky referred to them as 'the pride and glory' of the Russian Revolution. A fairly large percentage, perhaps even a majority, came from rural families and sympathized with the peasants' resentment of the hardships caused by the state's confiscation of their agricultural products. Anarchists and Left Socialist Revolutionaries found a sympathetic audience among the sailors, and by early 1921 they developed what has been called an 'anarcho-populist' program designed to fulfill the aspirations of the October Revolution of 1917. Among other things, they called on the government to grant 'full freedom of action in regard to the land' to the peasants, to organize new and secret elections of soviets, to permit freedom of speech and press to the workers and peasants, to liberate 'all political prisoners of socialist parties,' and, finally, to provide equal rations to all except those engaged in work detrimental to health, who deserved additional allowances. At a mass meeting, even many local Communists supported the demands. Then, on 2 March, the protesters formed a Provisional Revolutionary Committee to direct the movement and to conduct negotiations with the government. The demands of the insurgents were far-reaching: Paul Avrich, the foremost historian of these events, referred to them, with reason, as 'in many ways the most serious rebellion in Soviet history.' The most striking feature of the Kronstadt rebellion, as it became known, was that it was plainly a leftist movement that had nothing in common with the various right-wing groups still hoping to overthrow the government, which is precisely why the government found it so menacing. It could have led to a serious split among the supporters of the Bolshevik revolution, undermining the stability of the Communist regime.

The government appealed to the rebels to surrender, and when they refused, Trotsky organized an army to storm the fortress, the rebels' principal stronghold. It turned out to be a short conflict, although the insurgents resisted bravely. The government denounced the Kronstadt sailors and their supporters as counter-revolutionaries, and showed no mercy to its captives. No trial was ever held and hundreds, perhaps thousands, are estimated to have been summarily executed.

According to Lenin, the sailors' mutiny in Kronstadt 'lit up reality better than anything else.' Actually, he had decided even before the unrest that Russian economic policies needed to move in a fundamentally new direction. This became the central plank in the agenda of the Tenth Party Congress, whose meetings overlapped with the crushing of the rebellion. It was evident beyond any doubt that War Communism had failed to revive the economy. The new policies could succinctly be described as a partial return to capitalism; Lenin knew that the proposals would engender an outcry that he was betraying the cardinal principles of Marxism. To avoid rancorous debates and party divisions, he made a statement on the second day of the congress that laid the groundwork for the way the party and the country would be run for decades:

> We do not need any opposition now, comrades, it's not the time for it. Either here or over there with a rifle, but not with the opposition. It is no good reproaching me, it follows from the state of affairs. No more opposition now, comrades. And, in my view, the congress will have to draw the conclusion that the time has come to put an end to opposition, to put the lid on it, we have had enough opposition.

On the very last day of the congress, Lenin introduced a resolution calling for the immediate 'dissolution of all groups with separate platforms, on pain of immediate expulsion from the party.' The resolution also contained a section that remained secret for two years; it gave the Central Committee the authority to carry out the expulsions. Any other course was impossible, according to Lenin, because the country faced 'external dangers' too threatening to allow the formation within the party of groups that differed in the slightest degree from the party's official program. The congress voted overwhelmingly in favor of Lenin's recommendations.

The new rules on party discipline were designed to eliminate criticism and opposition to the New Economic Policy, which amounted to a fundamental change of direction for the Soviet Union. Although the government retained control over the large industries and the largest banks, much of the rest of the economy was to be privatized. In the countryside, compulsory requisitioning of food would end; instead, a tax would be imposed on farmers. In 1922, that tax was set at 10 percent of a farm's income, and the rest could be disposed of by peasants as they saw fit. In that same year, peasants were once again permitted to lease and hire labor. The purchase and sale of land continued to be illegal, but land could be leased and it became legal to lease machinery and cattle. In an effort to help poorer peasants, the government fostered the establishment of cooperatives.

For the first time in three years, trade became legal. Currency was introduced and the operations of the newly created State Bank were similar to those in capitalist countries. By 1924, all taxes in kind had been abolished and replaced by hard currency. In the industrial sector, the reforms were somewhat less radical. Both state-owned and privately owned establishments were permitted. However, the impact of private ownership of the means of production should not be overstated. True, within a few years, over 88 percent of industrial enterprises were in the hands of private citizens, but they employed only slightly more than 12 percent of the workforce. The government also decreed that private industry would be permitted to operate only if it did not constitute a threat to state-owned enterprises. That the state still played the preponderant role in the economy is demonstrated by the fact that while only 8.5 percent of the industrial enterprises remained under state control, they employed over 84 percent of the workforce.

The mixed economy proved to be a significant improvement over War Communism, despite some setbacks in its early period. Overall, by the winter of 1927–8, output in many sectors reached the level of 1913, the year before the outbreak of World War I, when civilian production began to decline. Two qualifications should be noted: since 1913, the population of Russia had increased from 139 million to 147 million, which means that the comparison between those two years is somewhat misleading. Moreover, because of the deterioration of the available machinery, the quality of goods produced in 1928 did not measure up to the standards of 1913. On the other hand, the wages of industrial workers in 1927 nearly equaled those of 1913, but if 'socialized wages,' such as health insurance and scholarships for education are taken into account, the workers in 1927 can be said to have been better off than their counterparts of fourteen years earlier.

Lenin's death and the struggle for power

Politically, the years of gradual economic improvement were a period of intense turbulence that boded ill for the future. The troubles began shortly after Lenin's death in January 1924, at the relatively young age of fifty-three. He had suffered a series of strokes, the first in May 1922, only a year after the New Economic Policy had been introduced. He continued to serve as leader of the country during his last two years, but his energy flagged and he no longer supervised the affairs of state with his former vigor. Still, he was so charismatic a figure in the Communist movement that no one openly challenged his authority. It was only during the last months of his life that he acknowledged that the country faced a serious political danger: one man in his entourage, Stalin, had, in a seemingly unobtrusive manner, amassed so much power that he would be in a position to impose his will on the Communist Party and the state. This deeply troubled Lenin, because he had concluded that Stalin was too rude and too ambitious to occupy so prominent a position. Shortly before his death, Lenin made these apprehensions explicit, by recommending in his testament that Stalin's wings be clipped. He also indicated that he regarded Trotsky, his right-hand man since 1917, as the most gifted member of the Central Committee, although he considered him to be overly self-confident and absorbed in the 'purely administrative side of affairs.' He described Bukharin as 'the most significant theoretician,' but regretted that he was weak in dialectics. Somehow, Stalin and his supporters succeeded in keeping the testament secret. It was not until 1926 that Max Eastman, an American writer then sympathetic to communism, managed to obtain a copy and publicize it. At about the same time as he composed the testament, Lenin also published an article in *Pravda* criticizing Stalin as a poor administrator and again accusing him of rudeness, but Lenin's attacks were phrased in vague language and therefore did not have a strong impact on leading party members.

Stalin's rise to political eminence is a fascinating story that should serve as a warning to people who believe that only charisma is the key to success in politics. Stalin was neither a particularly engaging person, nor a sparkling orator. Although he was intelligent, he did not have an original mind, and he never impressed associates as a man of profound insights. Yet he rose to the top position in Russia and remained in office as a dictatorial ruler for twenty-five years, until his death in 1953.

Stalin's outstanding qualities were shrewdness, a remarkable ability to conceal his ambitions, and ruthlessness, which he also managed to hide until he reached the pinnacle of power. Born in 1879 in Gori, Georgia, to a family of modest means—his father was a cobbler—he was destined for a career in the Orthodox

Church. At the age of ten, he was enrolled in an Orthodox seminary, where he studied until 1899, when he either decided to end his religious studies, or was expelled because he showed more interest in revolution than in Christianity—the documents are unclear. However, there is no doubt that he now devoted himself to the revolutionary cause. For the next fifteen years or so, he was a loyal and diligent member of the Marxist movement. He worked hard, but did not impress anyone as having exceptional abilities. His major achievement was the publication of an article on the nationality question from a Marxist standpoint, in which he adopted a dismissive attitude toward the principle of national autonomy, claiming that if minorities were granted autonomy in cultural affairs they would lose interest in political self-government. Within the inner circles of Russian Marxism, it was known that without Lenin's help the article would never have seen the light of day. In the years after 1903, when Bolshevism was emerging as an independent movement within Russian Marxism, Lenin viewed Stalin as a helpful and useful subordinate.

The Nationalities in the Russian Empire

In one important respect, the Russian Empire in the nineteenth century resembled the British Empire. In both cases, one national group—the British or the Russians—ruled over a vast area with a large population that was culturally, religiously, and economically diverse. Beyond that, the two empires were quite different. The British Empire comprised regions in various continents remote from the mother country, whereas the Russians dominated peoples in adjacent lands, stretching from the White Sea and the Arctic Ocean, to the Black and Caspian Seas, to Persia, Afghanistan, India, and China, and from the Baltic Sea to the Pacific Ocean. The absence of natural borders made it easier for the Russians to establish and maintain control over the neighboring lands, but, interestingly, the national minorities, just like the non-English peoples in the British Empire, did not lose their cultural identity, and eventually a fair number insisted on political independence.

The expansion of the Russian state began in the late fifteenth century and encountered remarkably little resistance, because the local people were weak economically, militarily, and politically. The expansion of the Great Russians, as they came to be known, continued until the late nineteenth century, by which time they represented a minority in the Empire, 44.3 percent of the total population of 122,666,500. True, other Slavic peoples were numerous: almost 18 percent were Ukrainians, over 6 percent were Poles, and slightly more than 4.5 percent were Belorussians, but at the time of the Revolution of 1917 these three minorities had developed their own cultures, and movements for political independence had gained considerable followings. To give a sense of the diversity of the population, it will suffice to mention just the most numerous among the 150 minorities: the Turkic people, who comprised close to 11 percent; the Finns, roughly 2.75 percent; the Jews, about 2.5 percent; the Lithuanians and Latvians, almost 2.5 percent; the Caucasian Mountain people, roughly 1.5 percent; the Georgians, slightly more than 1 percent; and, finally, the Armenians, close to 1 percent.

Although Christianity of the Eastern Orthodox persuasion was the state religion, with more adherents than any other faith, by the nineteenth century several other Christian denominations enjoyed sizable followings, as did Islam and Judaism. The form of rule imposed on the minorities by the Tsars varied, but overall Russian officials governed with an iron hand, and that kind of rule became especially severe in the late nineteenth and early twentieth centuries, which helps to explain why the national question became so critical in 1917.

Stalin came into his own after the Bolshevik seizure of power, in large part because he readily accepted party positions that more colorful and brilliant people shunned as purely administrative, and therefore not suitable for intellectuals. He held the position of Commissar of Nationalities, which endowed him with the authority to deal with the numerous economic problems of the minorities in Russia, close to 50 percent of the population. He was also Commissar of the Workers and Peasants Inspectorate, which gave him the power to investigate any official in the country suspected of wrongdoing. In the *Politburo*, a small group of top party leaders who really governed the country, he took on more of the day-to-day tasks of the party. In 1922, he was appointed General Secretary of the Central Committee, whose task it was to coordinate the work of its numerous branches. In that post, Stalin both set the agenda of the Politburo and supervised the implementation of its decisions. The General Secretary also handled the appointments and promotions of party functionaries. It soon became a position of enormous power; within a few years the General Secretary of the Communist Party in the Soviet Union, and in every other country with a Communist party, became the preeminent leader of the movement. Stalin never relinquished the title, even when he was the undisputed ruler of the Soviet Union. Stalin may not have been a philosopher of Marxism who came up with original and brilliant interpretations of socialist doctrine; *au fond*, he was a politician who knew how to transform administrative influence into political power. People with this gift are more likely to succeed as political leaders than people who have simply mastered the intricacies of Marxist dialectics.

Stalin had risen to the highest position in the country because he was extremely cunning and knew how to ingratiate himself with members of the Communist bureaucracy. He carefully cultivated contacts at all levels of the party, never tired of listening to people with complaints, and never gave the impression of harboring great personal ambition. Many of the minorities were economically disadvantaged and needed help and guidance from the authorities in Moscow, and Stalin always stood ready to oblige without requesting favors in return. Paradoxically, his apparent obscurity made him an ideal person for leadership in a political movement that derided the importance of individuals and emphasized the critical role of social forces in history. However, he and other twentieth-century dictators—such as Hitler and Mussolini—were to disprove that Marxist doctrine. They demonstrated that powerful individuals could exert enormous influence on the course of events: that they could, in fact, determine their countries' fate and that of many foreign countries.

That Stalin was not as unassertive a person as he appeared to the casual observer became evident in 1923, when he formed a triumvirate with Zinoviev and Kamenev, senior members of the Bolshevik Party, and members of the Politburo, to prevent Trotsky from assuming Lenin's position. The three men disposed of enough votes in the Politburo to make the critical decisions for the country, and since Politburo members were prohibited from discussing issues considered by the committee with outsiders, little was known in the country at large about the controversies in the highest circle of government. Trotsky, claiming that Russia was becoming dangerously 'bureaucratized,' called for discussion of national issues not only in the Central Committee, whose membership ranged from about seventy to one hundred, but also in the Communist Party as a whole. The triumvirate accused him of 'malevolence, personal ambition, neglect of government duties and so on.' Late in 1923, they relented somewhat and allowed limited debate within the party of major policy issues; it now became widely known that there were sharp divisions within the top ranks.

Kamenev and Zinoviev deluded themselves into believing that Stalin was their 'auxiliary' and consequently did not suspect that he coveted the top position in the party. He cleverly concealed his ambitions and concentrated on weakening Trotsky, clearly the front-runner to succeed Lenin, by sending many of the latter's leading supporters abroad on diplomatic missions. Stalin had the authority to do that because, as General Secretary, he controlled patronage. In that position, Stalin also was able to appoint party members to desirable positions and thus build a loyal following within the party.

At the Thirteenth Party Congress in May 1924, Trotsky realized that his opponents held the upper hand, and he therefore made an abject statement that not only revealed his own weakness but also the iron discipline demanded by the Communist Party:

The party in the last analysis is always right, because the party is the single historic instrument given to the proletariat for the solution of its fundamental problems. I have already said that in front of one's own party nothing could be easier than to acknowledge a mistake, nothing easier than to say: all my criticisms, my statements, my warnings, my protests—the whole thing was a mere mistake. I, however, comrades, cannot say that, because I do not think it. I know that one must not be right *against* the party. One can be right only with the party, and through the party, for history has created no other road for the realization of what is right. The English have a saying: 'Right or wrong—my country.' With far greater historic justification we may say: right or wrong, on separate particular issues, it is my party.

During 1924, the triumvirate deepened the conflict with Trotsky, attacking him on ideological grounds. They accused him of underestimating the peasantry, whom he allegedly considered bourgeois. He also made the mistake, according to Stalin, of contending that socialism could be fully established only after further growth of heavy industry, which would increase the size of the proletariat, the most reliable supporters of an egalitarian economic system. In taking this position, Trotsky, in the view of the triumvirate, committed the grievous mistake of rejecting Stalin's doctrine of 'socialism in one country' and continuing to insist on his own doctrine of 'permanent revolution.' Trotsky, it seemed to his opponents, was denigrating the Russian workers by contending that they could not achieve socialism by themselves and that the revolution would have to spread to the West to make possible its full realization in Russia.

On the other hand, Stalin's doctrine, based on the notion that Russia was so rich in raw materials that it did not have to wait for developments elsewhere to achieve its final goal, came to be widely accepted as sacred doctrine. It greatly bolstered the self-confidence of the masses, who felt reassured that their sacrifices would not be in vain. But within the top leadership there was much less certainty about the soundness of Stalin's doctrine. Even his close colleagues in the triumvirate, Zinoviev and Kamenev, did not take it seriously and thought that Stalin had expounded it simply as a weapon against Trotsky. When they realized that Stalin believed in his theory, they denounced it as an 'abandonment of traditional Bolshevism in favor of national communism.'

Many senior officials, however, approved of Stalin's doctrine because it was a powerful weapon against Trotsky. In 1925, the Politburo took several measures to clip Trotsky's wings. He was forced to resign from the Commissariat of War; realizing his political weakness, he made no effort to win support within the party or the army and for an entire year stayed out of all public debates. With Trotsky neutralized, Stalin increasingly disregarded Zinoviev and Kamenev. He formed a new alliance with Bukharin, M. I. Rykov, and K. Y. Tomsky and, since the Politburo had been increased in size from five to seven, he could again count on a majority. Late in 1925, at the Fourteenth Party Congress, Stalin persuaded the members to enlarge the Politburo to ten. By adding V. M. Molotov, K. Y. Voroshilov, and M. I. Kalinin to the august body, Stalin could count on the support of three additional senior party members. Amazingly, the officials at the highest level of the party did not realize that Stalin was manipulating the system to enhance his own power.

Stalin as Supreme Leader

Late in 1925, a debate began over the future of the New Economic Policy, which had been introduced in 1921, and had markedly improved the national economy. It did not take long for the debate to intersect with the political struggles following

Lenin's death, which now became fiercer than ever, and more complicated. The Left, led by Zinoviev and Kamenev, argued that industrial production had not grown fast enough and that the peasants were selling too few products on the market. Only if industrial goods were produced at lower cost would the peasants be encouraged to boost production so they could acquire those goods. The Left also feared the growing economic power of the landed peasants, who might soon become so strong a force that they would be able to introduce political changes that would undermine the Communist system. Zinoviev and Kamenev proposed the establishment of collective farms to weaken private farmers as an economic and political force. They also believed that socialist revolutions on the Russian model were still possible in the West; such a development, they insisted, would bolster the Soviet Union.

On the other hand, Bukharin, now the leader of the right wing of the Communist Party, warned that the Left's program of rapid industrialization could be introduced only by increasing taxes on private enterprises and private farmers, which would wreak havoc on the economy, already in a precarious condition, and possibly bring back the hardships endured by the country during the period of War Communism. He suggested that the government adopt the slogan 'enrich yourselves, accumulate, develop your economy', which harked back to the days of F. P. G. Guizot, the prime minister of France in 1847–8, who gave that advice to citizens interested in securing the right to vote. In Bukharin's view, so long as the Communists controlled industry, transportation, and banking, there was no danger that socialism would be undermined if his proposals were adopted. In contrast to the Left, Bukharin discounted the likelihood of revolutions breaking out in the West. In his view, Russia had to concentrate on building 'socialism in one country.'

In 1925, Stalin supported the position of the Right, although he did not involve himself in the theoretical debates. Taxes on agricultural products were reduced and the government made it easier for farmers to lease land and hire labor. Stalin seized the opportunity to criticize Zinoviev and Kamenev, leaders of the Left, but for the time being leveled no attacks on Trotsky. His aim, clearly, was to prevent the three men from forming a political alliance. At the same time, he weakened Zinoviev by removing many of his followers from important party positions. He also began to denigrate both Zinoviev and Kamenev, labeling them 'deserters' and 'strikebreakers' for having opposed the Bolshevik seizure of power in 1917. In the spring of 1926, the two formed an alliance with their former enemy, Trotsky, but it was a meaningless gesture, since Stalin had already undermined their authority in the party. He further weakened all three by revealing the nasty things they had said about each other. Kamenev and Zinoviev retaliated by describing Stalin as 'a sly, revengeful sadist, obsessed with vanity and a lust for power.' However, many in the party did not find their indictment of the General Secretary convincing, because they failed to explain why they had worked so closely with such a despicable person. As is often the case in political conflicts, the struggles among the Russian leaders were motivated as much by a drive for personal power and prestige as by differences over doctrine.

Stalin emerged the victor because he outwitted his rivals, who were remarkably inept politicians. To the party at large, he gave the impression of being a soft-spoken, mild-mannered, moderate politician, a pose that enabled him to gain the support of a majority in the highest echelons of the party, which he used to deal harshly with his opponents. In 1926, he managed to oust Zinoviev and Trotsky from the Politburo, and a year later arranged their expulsion from the Central Committee. In November 1927, Trotsky and Zinoviev demonstrated their disapproval of Stalin by leading a separate group of their followers in the celebration of the tenth anniversary of the revolution. They were immediately punished with expulsion from the Communist Party, and a month later, seventy-five additional senior Communists were kicked out. Trotsky received an even more severe punishment: he was deported to Alma Ata, a city near the Chinese border. Early in 1929, Stalin had him banished from the Soviet Union. Zinoviev and Kamenev, by now well-known for their flexibility, publicly recanted their 'heretical' views, and were readmitted to the party, but they were humiliated, and never regained their previous positions.

In the meantime, Stalin continued to play off one group against another in the Central Committee until he emerged as the undisputed leader of the Communist Party and the dictator of the country. On his fiftieth birthday, on 21 December 1929, his supporters initiated a campaign of adulation. His bust was displayed in numerous places throughout the country, marking the initiation of the cult of personality that would be a central feature of the political system for the next twenty-four years. In much of the world, 'Stalinism' now became synonymous with Soviet socialism, and soon inspired more dread than the term 'Leninism.'

7

Stalin's completion of the revolution

Some historians have referred to Stalin's economic and political policies as a second revolution—often described as a 'revolution from above'—because he abandoned the New Economic Policy, vastly increased the state's role in the national economy, and sought to eliminate inequality of income. Stalin and his supporters claimed, correctly, that they were finally establishing the kind of socio-economic system envisioned by Marx and his earliest supporters.

There can be no doubt about the radicalism of Stalin's policies and achievements. Within a few years, the Soviet Union became an industrial state and a majority of the population could be classified as proletarian. Industry was tightly controlled by the government, which saw to it that the pay scale of workers would not encompass large differences. At the same time, the government introduced a program of collectivization of agriculture, which meant the elimination of privately-owned farms. The peasants, too, were provided with incomes that did not vary greatly from one to another.

Although these changes were far-reaching, it is not self-evident that they constituted a second revolution. They may more accurately be seen as the fulfillment of Lenin's plans and those of the Bolshevik Party generally in 1917–18. In its basic thrust, collectivization of agriculture was not all that far removed from War Communism, the economic system imposed on the Soviet Union between 1918 and 1921. At that time, economic power was also concentrated in the hands of the central government. Lenin abandoned his radical economic program not because he had changed his mind about its legitimacy or desirability, but because the economy had declined to a dangerous level. Whether or not he intended the partial return to capitalism that year to be permanent is not clear, but Stalin's accomplishment in the economic sphere did not contradict Lenin's earlier dreams for Russia and for the rest of the world.

In the political sphere, Stalin's policies also did not constitute a revolution. Although far more crude and brutal than Lenin, Stalin, like his master in 1921, sought to put a halt to all opposition to both his policies and his rule. Stalin pursued this goal with inordinate ruthlessness, and produced a political order unprecedented for the degree of governmental control over society in virtually all its aspects. In addition, Russia or, more accurately, the Soviet Union, became a military power of the first rank after World War II, widely feared in much of the world. To use Reed's evocative expression, forty years after 1917, the Russian Revolution continued to shake the world.

The Five-Year Plan

In 1927, few people in the Soviet Union wanted or expected an upheaval that would once again thrust the country into turmoil, and disrupt the lives of millions of citizens. As already noted, the standard of living of most people approached that of 1913, and peasants owned more land than in the prewar years. True, the people did not enjoy political freedom, but they also did not suffer from overbearing political oppression. It seemed to many that ten years of power had moderated the Communists, who would now concentrate on a gradual strengthening of the industrial sector of the economy.

However, Stalin was moved, by both practical and political considerations, to embark on a new course. By 1927, the revival of the large-scale industry that had existed in 1917 seemed to have run its course; any further increase in production would require new policies. The Soviet Union could try to import new machinery, but for that it would have to export agricultural goods. Yet to increase the agricultural surplus, more industry would be needed to produce machinery for farmers. It was a vicious circle that Soviet leaders believed could be broken only by substantially increasing production and reducing consumption, which would leave sufficient capital for the development of industry. That became the underlying principle of the Five-Year Plans.

These considerations fitted in well with Stalin's political concerns. In 1925, he had adopted the slogan 'socialism in one country,' but under the New Economic Policy the country appeared to be drifting away from socialism. Stalin feared that the peasants were developing into a powerful force and in time would press for a full restoration of capitalism. He therefore launched a campaign against the so-called *kulaks* (fists), the well-to-do peasants who made up no more than 3.9 percent of the population in the agrarian regions of the country. There was no clear definition of kulak; in the pre-1917 era, the word was applied to peasants who were better off than most, often rich enough to engage in money-lending and mortgaging. In the 1920s, the term referred to any peasant who owned one of the larger farms, draft animals, and machinery, and who employed some workers. It has been estimated that in 1927, the kulaks produced only 13 percent of the country's grain; 85 percent was produced by middle-income and poorer peasants.

Seventy-five percent of the peasants still lived in communes, which were more important centers of administration than the soviets or cooperatives. According to official statistics, the 2,300 soviets in the countryside disposed of a total budget of about sixteen million rubles, whereas the budget of various peasant associations in the entire country amounted to eighty million rubles. Moreover, the kulaks tended to serve as leaders of local organizations. In short, in the ten years since the revolution the Communist Party had failed to place its loyal followers in key positions in the villages, a state of affairs the government considered a potential threat to its control of the country.

The Commune

The commune (*mir* or *obshchina* in Russian) was the dominant economic and social institution of most peasants in Russia. It was apparently founded in the fourteenth century by groups of peasants who believed that cooperative farming would promote efficiency and bring about a fair and just way of organizing the local economy. Actually, the arrangements in about 80 percent of the communes severely hindered efficiency. The land was periodically redistributed to maintain equality of allotments for peasant families, whose size would naturally vary over the years. In many communes the land was divided into strips, to guarantee that all the peasants had a share of both the best and the least productive land. As a result, peasants had to spend a considerable amount of time walking from one to another of their holdings, a further drag on efficiency.

There was thus no tradition of private ownership of land among the bulk of the country's population, and the peasants had no incentive to make long-range improvements on their holdings. Many socialists, among them Karl Marx, believed that this communal arrangement in vast regions of Russia would predispose the peasants, who had never owned property, to support socialism. Marx even suggested that because of the peasants' experience with the commune Russia might be able to skip the phase of capitalism altogether and move directly into socialism. It turned out, however, that although the Russian peasants appreciated many of the functions of the commune, they shared the hopes of farmers in other countries; they wanted to own the land that afforded them their livelihood.

The authorities in Moscow were also troubled by the peasants' failure to abandon their devotion to the Orthodox Church, which to Communists symbolized 'the rot of tsarism.' Apparently, in 1928 alone some 560 new communities of Orthodox believers were formed, and in the Ukraine the number of priests greatly increased.

In 1927, the government faced another alarming development, a significant decline in the amount of grain reaching urban centers. A major reason for the decline was that in comparison to the prewar period, most of the grain for the market was now produced not by landlords and kulaks but by middle-income and poorer peasants, who were living better and consuming a larger portion of their crops. During the 1920s, total agrarian production had increased by some 62 percent, but the portion sent to market had grown only by 26.3 percent. There is no evidence to support the suspicion among the left wing of the Communist Party that the peasants were deliberately holding back deliveries to the cities to enhance their political influence, but the Communist Left, and Stalin, found no other explanation convincing.

Moreover, Stalin believed that rapid industrialization was necessary to prepare the Soviet Union for possible military conflict against Western powers determined to crush the socialist experiment. In 1926, relations between the Soviet Union and Britain had turned especially tense, because Soviet officials had openly supported the British coal miners who, at the time, were engaged in a bitter strike. In 1927, Britain broke off diplomatic relations with the Soviet Union.

Ideological considerations seem to have been paramount. The Politburo charged *Gosplan* (the State Planning Commission, established in 1921) with the task of drawing up a plan for restructuring the economy. The task was monumental; Gosplan quickly came up with precise, all-embracing, and startlingly ambitious goals. A key aspect of the plan was to turn every worker into an employee of the state. For a true believer in socialism, no goal was more sacrosanct.

Gosplan formulated a Five-Year Plan that set specific goals for every sector of the economy: industry as a whole was to increase production by 235.9 percent; heavy industry was to reach an even larger increase, 279.2 percent. Output of pig iron was to be virtually tripled, coal doubled, and electric power was to increase fourfold. Agriculture was assigned a more moderate increase, 150 percent. In addition, the government announced that the cost of industrial goods would be reduced by 35 percent, but wholesale prices would be reduced by only 24 percent, leaving a substantial profit for investment. Within two years, in June 1930, the government's enthusiasm reached the level of euphoria. Even though it had become clear that unrealistic targets had been projected, Stalin claimed that the plan would be fulfilled in four years, not five.

In fact, the economic surge turned out to be chaotic and often ineffective; in some regions, factories had been built, but there were not enough machines to fill them, and it frequently turned out that the new enterprises lacked enough skilled workers to run the machines. None of the projected goals was reached, and in several sectors of the economy the shortfalls were significant.

Nevertheless, in certain respects the results of the Five-Year Plan were impressive. The Soviet Union was on the road to being transformed into a major industrial power. The country could boast of having developed entirely new industries that produced tractors, automobiles, agricultural machinery, and airplanes. Perhaps the most striking statistic to support this conclusion is that by 1932 the labor force had risen to 22.8 million, about seven million more than had been projected. Another measure of the extent of the change in the economy is indicated by the fact that between 1928 and 1932 industrial output rose from 48 percent to 70 percent of the country's total production of goods.

The Soviet people paid a heavy price for these achievements, and many economists believe that similar results could have been achieved without the terrible pain. The peasants suffered the most. Gosplan decided that the only way to secure enough capital and workers for industrialization was to abolish individual farms and replace them with collective farms. Initially, the plan was to achieve collectivization through a voluntary process, but it soon became clear that most peasants did not want to give up their farms. The state therefore forced peasants into the collectives, if necessary by bayonet or bullet. For Stalin, collectivization was to achieve the ultimate goal of Bolshevism. As he put it in 1928, 'Either we go backward to capitalism, or we go forward to socialism …' In destroying the commune and with it the traditional rural culture, Stalin was in effect completing the revolution that Lenin had started in 1917.

Many of the peasants were so infuriated that before leaving their farms they killed their livestock and burned their crops. Within two years, by March 1930, about 55 percent of all peasant families were reported as having been collectivized, but even Stalin claimed to recognize the brutality of the process. Early in 1933, he published an article, *Dizzy with Success*, in which he declared that collectivization could not be imposed by force. He blamed the violence and chaos in the villages on lower Communist Party officials. By May, the number of peasant families in collectives actually dropped from fourteen to six million. Soon, the process of collectivization was resumed at a somewhat more gradual pace, and by 1932, 60 percent of all families belonged to collectives.

For the peasants, and for the country at large, collectivization turned out to be a disaster. In the space of two years, from 1929 to 1931, the number of cattle in the Soviet Union dropped by one-third, and the number of sheep and goats by one-half, as did the number of horses. It has been estimated by scholars that during the implementation of the agrarian policy, and the ensuing famine of 1932–3 in the Ukraine, the northern Caucasus, the Volga region, Kazakhstan, and the West Siberian Plain, at least five million peasants lost their lives.

Realizing the enormity of the havoc in the countryside, the government made some concessions to the peasants. Instead of forcing them into the preferred type of collective, the state farm (*sovkhoz*), in which peasants worked full-time on the commonly held land, it gave them the option of entering a *kolkhoz*, in which the peasants divided their working time between their own small plots and the land controlled by the collective. Most collectives fell into the latter category. Ironically, this twofold arrangement not only deviated from the orthodox principles of Communism, but also demonstrated the effectiveness of economic incentives. Peasants in the kolkhozy would work leisurely during the sixty to one hundred days they devoted to the collectivized land and preserve their energy for their own plots, the proceeds of which they could sell directly to consumers. It was only at the end of the 1930s that the harvests of farms surpassed those of the late 1920s. During the next five decades—for as long as the Soviet Union existed—agricultural productivity remained very low, as did the quality of food products, and since the transportation system was primitive, a significant percentage of the produce rotted before it ever reached the market. The consensus among historians of the Soviet Union is that Stalin's agrarian policies were a catastrophic failure.

Although industrial workers ranked high in the esteem of the government, the conditions under which they lived were not markedly better than those of the peasants. To imbue factory employees with the necessary work habits, early in the 1930s the government introduced rigid discipline. For example, factory managers controlled the issuance of ration cards, which until 1935 were required for the purchase of food and manufactured goods. Workers dismissed from their jobs were deprived of their cards, and often also their home, which was under the enterprise's control. After 1932, if workers were absent from their jobs for a single day without good reason, factory managers were directed to dismiss them and deprive them of their homes. The growing intrusion of the state in the affairs of the citizens was an integral aspect of Stalin's attempt to reorganize Soviet society from above and thus marked a turn toward a new political system that is often classified as totalitarianism.

The Soviet Union as a totalitarian state

Over the past few decades, scholars have argued passionately over the legitimacy of designating the Soviet Union as *totalitarian*. Many claim that the term is imprecise and was invented to create a 'counter-ideology' for the dual purpose of denigrating and defeating Communism. Mussolini had used the word in 1925, when he proudly claimed to be turning Italy into a *totalitarian* state, by which he meant that it would be guided by the rather vague dogma of: 'Everything for the state, nothing outside the state, nothing against the state.' By the 1930s, the term was occasionally used in the press, and by diplomats, to describe the political systems of Communism and Nazism. It became popular among academics only after the 1951 publication of Hannah Arendt's famous book, *The Origins of Totalitarianism*, in which she sought to describe the nature and sources of both Communism and Nazism. Arendt has never been described as an ardent ideologue of anti-Communism.

In 1969, the English scholar Leonard Schapiro described what he called the main contours of the political systems of the Soviet Union, Nazi Germany, and fascist Italy, all of which he believed fell under the rubric of totalitarianism. In the first place, in all three countries the Leader was preeminent, so much so that his word on a wide range of subjects, not merely on politics, was even more important than established party doctrine. Second, the legal order depended not on any established rules but on the pronouncements of the Leader. Opponents, or presumed opponents, of the political order were punished without even the pretense of respect for the rule of law. Third, the Leader, or those acting on his behalf, exercised control over the 'area of private morality' and the nation's cultural institutions. Fourth, the totalitarian leader maintained the fiction of democratic rule by seeking mass support for his policies, either by staged elections or mass demonstrations. Finally, in totalitarian systems, there was 'a fever of constant mobilization. Everyone is at all times being galvanized, dragooned, exhorted, shamed or compelled to act for some end or other.'

Thus defined, totalitarianism seems to be an accurate description of the political system in the Soviet Union after Stalin's assumption of power. To be sure, there were differences between Communism and Nazism on ultimate goals and on the social support upon which they relied. Racism was central to Hitler's ideology, which was not true of Stalin's. Hitler did not break up the upper classes, which had held powerful positions in Germany before 1933. By contrast, the Communists carried out their stated policy of depriving the traditional upper classes of their privileges. The modes of rule that the Communists and Fascists used to attain their ultimate goals were not all that different. Both imposed absolute dictatorships on their countries, both failed to heed moral scruples in imposing their wills on the nation, and both sought to control every facet of the country's social and cultural life, although it should be kept in mind that in none of the totalitarian countries did the political leadership fully attain its goals. A fair number of citizens in the Soviet Union, as in Nazi Germany and Fascist Italy, refused to go along with the demands of the authorities. These people held on to their own views and wherever possible courageously ignored the police of a state they considered immoral, unjust, or ineffective. Readers who find the term *totalitarianism* inappropriate might find the following description of the Stalinist regime more acceptable: it was a brutal, all-embracing dictatorship. In the final analysis, for the student of the Soviet Union it is important to understand how it functioned, not the name that scholars assign to it.

Stalin was the undisputed leader of the Soviet Union. He controlled the Communist Party, the single most powerful institution for implementing his economic and cultural policies. He controlled the army, as well as the dreaded secret police, and he acted as arbiter of disputes over ideology and cultural issues. He was not a flamboyant ruler in the style of Hitler or Mussolini, but he knew how to promote his cult of personality. His photograph appeared in numerous locations throughout the Soviet Union. Although he did not issue a formal edict claiming infallibility, his word—on politics, art, films, literature, and even science—was taken by many people to be indisputable. Very few in the Soviet Union had not heard of his genius in every walk of life, and even fewer did not fear him.

To many in the political class in the West, Communism now became an anathema, not only because it stood for the elimination of private property in the means of production, but also because it had created a political order that discarded the principles of liberalism, popular rule, and the rule of law, all of which were regarded as fundamental in Western democracies.

The political structure of the Soviet Union, much of it created in the late 1920s and 1930s, was designed to keep the levers of power in all areas of public life in the hands of the central authorities in Moscow, which in turn were subservient to Stalin. From time to time, the structure was altered—there were even three constitutions, adopted in 1924, 1936, and 1977—but it would be pointless to describe them in detail, since the changes did not affect the exercise of power. It will suffice to name the main political institutions and briefly mention their functions. However, the reader should keep in mind that the institutions do not bear any resemblance to those in Western democracies, since power was concentrated in the hands of the party leaders who were not freely elected by the people.

At the base of the entire system was the soviet at the local level, which was elected by universal, equal, and secret suffrage;

citizens began to vote at the age of eighteen. Although provision was made for wide participation in the selection of candidates for public office, the functionaries in the Communist Party played a critical role in this process. It was very unlikely that people critical of, or simply indifferent to, the prevailing regime would be nominated for a seat in a soviet.

The soviets in the cities and villages exercised authority over local matters, such as the maintenance of order, local economic and cultural institutions, the formulation of budgets, and the election of judges. In fact, the sphere of authority of these soviets was severely limited, because they constituted the base of an elaborate hierarchy of soviets; the higher the soviet the more political influence it exerted. There were soviets in geographical regions, in the autonomous republics, and, finally, there was the Supreme Soviet in Moscow, which was by far the most powerful. It was officially designated as the 'embodiment of all authority, legislative, executive and judicial.' It was elected by direct suffrage for four years, but its powers were not those of a parliament or congress in Western countries. In practice, the Presidium, often referred to as a 'collective president,' consisting of thirty-seven members, issued decrees without consulting the Supreme Soviet, which had a membership of about fifteen hundred. According to the Constitution of 1936, the Council of Ministers was to serve simply as an executive-administrative organ and was to be subordinate to the legislature, the Supreme Soviet, which chose ministers, but here, too, practice differed from theory. In fact, the Council of Ministers was a very powerful political institution because it administered the economy, the military services, and the foreign policy establishment. Finally, the ministers were at all times expected to heed the wishes of the Politburo of the Communist Party; this was generally not an issue, since virtually all ministers were also senior members of the party and were not inclined to question its leader.

To grasp the essence of the Soviet system of rule, it is useful to recall the thesis advanced by Merle Fainsod in 1953, in his classic work *How Russia Is Ruled*. Fainsod argued that the regime created under Stalin rested on three pillars: the Communist Party, which supervised the indoctrination of the masses and controlled 'the entire social order'; the secret police, which resorted to terror to guard against the emergence of any opposition to the regime; and the political and social elite, which occupied the most important positions in the administration, the economy, the army, and the cultural and scientific institutions. Known as the *nomenklatura* in Russian, the members of this group were well-paid, and the state bestowed many honors on them. They shopped at special stores, well-stocked with low-priced food and other goods, which were not available to the rest of the population. The authorities attempted, without much success, to conceal these stores; no one could enter them without a special identity card, but many citizens knew their location and knew what kind of business was conducted within.

The Communist Party, dubbed by the leaders of the Soviet Union as the 'vanguard of the proletariat,' was charged with the task of guiding the masses. In fact, the party assumed responsibility for directing every institution in the Soviet Union. As Stalin put it, the party was to issue the 'guiding directions' on policies, which were then to be implemented by the soviets. To assure itself of the loyalty of the soviets, the government carefully controlled the elections. Thus, only one candidate was presented to voters, who then faced the choice of accepting the party's candidate or of entering a booth, in full view of party members, to replace the party's choice with their own. Not many citizens were willing to take that risk.

Membership in the Communist Party was a privilege restricted to people who had proven their loyalty to the political system. To assure itself of a steady supply of reliable members, the party started the screening process early in the lives of Soviet citizens. Political education began in kindergarten, where children were called Little Octobrists; at the age of nine, they joined the Young Pioneers, and their political education became more rigorous. Almost all children became Pioneers, but at the age of fourteen they underwent careful screening before being admitted to the Komsomol, the movement that catered to young people until the age of twenty-six. Members of the Komsomol received more advanced political training and were expected to serve as model Soviet citizens. Many youngsters eagerly applied for membership because they knew that service for the party, which was very demanding, would greatly enhance their chances of successful careers. The Komsomol served as the pool from which individuals were selected for full membership in the Communist Party, a privilege not enjoyed by many. In 1933, party membership reached three and a half million out of a total population of about 160 million. However, for reasons that will become clear, party membership fluctuated considerably throughout the 1930s.

Hierarchically organized, the party became a reliable tool of the central authorities in Moscow. Its guiding principle was *democratic centralism,* which in practice meant far greater emphasis on centralism than on democracy. True, all party institutions were to be elected and each one was required to issue periodic reports on its work. Strict 'party discipline' was enforced: the decisions of the higher bodies in the hierarchy were binding and minorities in every party organization were at all times required to subordinate their wishes to those of the majority. Also, no one in the lower ranks of the party hierarchy was permitted to criticize the decisions of the higher bodies.

Although very important in the running of state affairs, the party by itself could not ensure the smooth implementation of Stalin's policies. The vast majority of its members held daytime jobs and could devote only evenings and weekends to political work. The government needed cadres of full-time party workers, *apparatchiki* or party functionaries, whose sole professional task was to oversee the smooth implementation of orders from Moscow. It has been estimated that in 1925 there were about 25,000 full-time functionaries, a number that rose to about 194,000 by 1952. They passed on to the rank and file the wishes of the top political leadership in Moscow, and made recommendations for the appointment and promotion of people considered able and reliable not only in the party hierarchy but also in the economic sphere, trade unions, agriculture, and so on. To ensure their absolute loyalty, the leadership rewarded these functionaries with salaries much higher—in some cases 50 percent higher—than those of employees in comparable positions in other branches of the government.

The Communist rulers paid special attention to the establishment of new educational institutions. By 1928, over forty thousand party schools, study groups, and organized courses had been created to educate the people in the principles of Marxism and to prepare them for possible membership in the Communist Party. At the same time, party cells were formed in universities, but in higher education the government had to exercise a degree of caution. Not enough trained scholars were available to quickly turn the universities into servants of the state. A start was made in 1921, when the Red Professors' Institute was established, for the purpose of producing university lecturers committed to Communism. Within three years, ten 'Communist universities' were created and by 1928 the number had risen to nineteen; all told, there were eighty-four thousand students in these institutions, which specialized in the social sciences, history, and philosophy.

In sum, during the years of the first Five-Year Plan, the Communist Party increased its control of all walks of the country's life. This was considered important to enable the authorities to whip up enthusiasm for the economic transformation of the Soviet Union. As already suggested, the system of control was never as effective as the authorities hoped; recent scholarship has shown that a number of people succeeded in ignoring or violating the rules handed down from above, but such behavior was risky. Still, it should be kept in mind that the aims of the Soviet rulers were never fully achieved.

State terror

The political and economic changes that Stalin engineered came at a heavy price; the imposition on the Soviet Union of a dictatorship more authoritarian and ruthless than that of the Tsars. It is still something of a puzzle why after 1933 Stalin felt the need to institute a regime of terror so sweeping and indiscriminate that it left few families in the Soviet Union untouched. No doubt, he had convinced himself that force would be needed to persuade the people to accept his vision of socialism. He sought an ideal society and to reach that goal, any means were acceptable. However, as will become clear, his terror went far beyond affecting only the lives of people who disagreed with him on how to reach socialism. It also affected people who shared his ultimate goal and even approved of the means he applied to achieve them.

Scholars have disagreed on the number of people who suffered from state terrorism, but there is now agreement that it ran into many hundreds of thousands and almost certainly into millions. The most prominent victim was Leon Trotsky, a hero in 1917 and Lenin's second-in-command, but in the 1920s, Stalin's most prominent rival for the party's leadership. His fate is a gripping story and provides clear insight into Stalin's ruthlessness.

Trotsky was exiled to Alma Ata, Kazakhstan in 1928. After spending a year in domestic exile in that remote city, he was forced to leave the Soviet Union in 1929. He first went to Turkey, where he spent four years, then to Norway, France, and finally, in 1936, to Mexico. The governments of the first three countries did not want him as a permanent resident, for fear that he would cause social unrest. In Mexico, sympathizers with the

Communist cause—particularly the artist Diego Rivera—gladly welcomed him and provided him with a home in a lovely area in the countryside near Mexico City. Stalin, who by this time had become obsessed with his own importance, still feared Trotsky, perhaps because he knew that his long-time enemy was so much more gifted a theorist, writer, and orator that he might stage a political comeback; or perhaps Stalin simply could not bear the thought that the man he considered his mortal enemy was still alive and continued to attract followers, especially among the educated elite in the West. Whatever the reason, in August 1940 a Spanish Communist, under orders from the Soviet secret police, gained entrance to Trotsky's study and hacked at his skull with an axe, killing the man who had been Lenin's closest ally from 1917 to 1924. The murderer received a twenty-year prison sentence, but Stalin bestowed an honor upon him *in absentia*.

The murder of Trotsky shocked and frightened his followers and stunned many in the West, who did not expect this sort of lawlessness and brutality from what was still widely believed to be a progressive state. The details of the regime's ruthlessness against its own people trickled out to the West gradually, but they were so gruesome that it took time for them to be absorbed. By the early 1940s, so much information was available that only the Soviet Union's most ardent supporters dared deny that state terror was a central feature of Soviet Communism.

It is worth noting that the two conditions necessary for a 'legal order' did not exist in the Soviet Union. The judiciary was not independent; on the contrary, it was very much under the control of the Communist Party. Moreover, there were no fixed rules governing the conduct of executive power. Even during the 1920s, the courts exercised vast discretionary power in dealing with anyone suspected of opposition to the government. Articles II and X of the Criminal Code were so broad in permitting judges to mete out punishment to anyone accused of 'socially dangerous' acts that they afforded little protection to the accused.

A socially dangerous act was defined as one that 'menaces the stability of the dictatorship of the proletariat' or 'is an obstacle to the development of socialism, or disorganizes social relations, even where such an act is not specifically foreseen by the Code.' It was the application of such broad powers by the government that characterized what has come to be known as the 'Great Terror.'

In addition, the Stalinist leadership offered two justifications for the terror that, in more or less the same form, had been rehearsed by its practitioners ever since the French Revolution of 1789: the revolution is the ultimate good, because its aim is to improve the lot of the people, and whatever is done to support it is therefore lawful; the Soviet Union must be on guard at all times because the counterrevolutionary forces were determined to crush Communism—as was most clearly evidenced by what the Communists called the 'capitalist encirclement' of the Soviet Union.

It took the Bolsheviks only weeks—until 7 December, 1917—to establish a secret police, known as the *Cheka*, to cope with domestic enemies. Initially, the Cheka's charge was confined to investigating criminal actions against the regime, but very soon it was granted the power to carry out 'executive actions,' which meant that, without normal judicial proceedings, it could conduct 'unrestricted searches,' send people to forced labor camps, and even execute prisoners considered guilty of serious crimes. The name of the Cheka changed several times, apparently to give the impression that its mode of operation had changed. During the period when it was most active, from 1934 until 1946, it was known as the NKVD.

The secret police relied on informers in various organizations of Soviet society—large factories, universities, schools, trade unions, and the armed forces. The NKVD also encouraged citizens to submit anonymous denunciations of individuals suspected of actions harmful to the state. When such people were rounded up by the police, the trials, if they were held at all, took place before military tribunals of the Supreme Court. The defendants were not permitted to be represented by legal counsel and no witnesses were called in their defense.

The Stalinist terror reached its apogee in the mid-1930s, shortly after the assassination on 1 December 1934, in Leningrad (the re-named Petrograd), of Sergei Kirov, the head of the local party organization, who was widely believed to be Stalin's heir. Nikolaev, the assassin, was known to be a follower of Zinoviev, a leading opponent of Stalin in the 1920s. There has been speculation, although no definitive proof, that Stalin may have been the person who gave the orders to kill Kirov, because he seemed to be developing into a rival for the top post in the party.

Be that as it may, within hours of the murder, the Central Executive Committee of the party published a decree depriving people suspected of committing an act of terror of almost all rights of judicial defense. At the same time, the Communist Party issued a secret order calling for speedy trials of anyone accused of terrorism; once the investigation was completed, the suspects were to be executed immediately. In mid-January 1935, Zinoviev, Kamenev, and several other leading Communists who had supported the opposition were charged as criminals, the first time this had been done to prominent members of the Communist Party. The accused were put on trial in January 1935, but the prosecutor could not prove his case, even though the prisoners acknowledged 'general political responsibility' for the murder of Kirov. Zinoviev was sentenced to ten years in prison and Kamenev to five. A year and a half later, they were tried again, and this time confessed to having planned the murder and also to having planned to assassinate Stalin. Found guilty, they were immediately shot.

The police then made more arrests of leading Communists (Rykov, Bukharin, Tomsky, and others). They were accused of plotting to dismember the Soviet Union, a preposterous charge against undyingly loyal Marxists and passionate supporters of the Communist revolution. Many issued confessions, which has puzzled historians and political scientists ever since. One explanation that received wide approval was suggested by the novelist Arthur Koestler: that the accused were such staunch party members that they offered confessions as a last service to a noble cause. They feared that if they publicly defended themselves and accused Stalin and his henchmen of murdering loyal Communists, they would split the Marxist movement and endanger the socialist state. Another explanation for their abject behavior may be more convincing: that they had been beaten down by their long isolation, had been promised that they would be spared the death sentence, and warned that their families would be harmed if they did not plead guilty as charged. Whatever might have transpired behind the scenes, we know that they were all executed.

For Stalin, who had come to believe in his indispensability and the treachery of anyone who uttered a word of doubt about his policies, these trials were only the beginning of a campaign to root out all who might question his absolute authority. He initiated a purge of the Communist Party and major public institutions so vast that only its main features can be mentioned in this account. A sizable portion of those accused were shot without trial, but most received prison sentences ranging from five to ten years and were sent to one of the numerous labor camps.

A startling aspect of the government terror was that it reached a huge number of people who had worked loyally for the regime and many who had held positions at the highest levels of government service, such as Kamenev and Zinoviev. In June 1937, Stalin's subordinates initiated a purge of the military forces, which one might have assumed would be sacrosanct, given the growing threat of a rapidly rearming Nazi Germany. Three out of five marshals, thirteen of fifteen army commanders, fifty-seven of eighty-five corps commanders, 110 of 195 division commanders, 220 of 406 brigade commanders, all eleven vice commissars of war, seventy-five of eighty members of the Supreme Military

Council, 90 percent of all generals, and 80 percent of all colonels were arrested and killed.

The decimation of the political elite was no less astonishing: of 1,966 voting and nonvoting delegates at the Seventeenth Party Congress in 1932, 1,108, more than half, were taken into custody and charged with counterrevolutionary crimes. During a two-year period from 1937 to 1938, several hundreds of thousands of officials in the Communist Party were dismissed; many were shot without trial.

Various explanations can be given for the wholesale slaughter of faithful Communists, but the bloodletting was so capricious and harmful to the state that none seems entirely convincing. The decrees on the purges, recently published, claimed that they were directed to a large extent at categories of people who were suspected of harboring strong anti-Bolshevik views, such as former kulaks, ethnic minorities, and people who had at one time supported political parties hostile to Communism. Some commentators have suggested that the trials of former political leaders, and the purges of the Communist Party, enabled Stalin to divert attention from the economic failings of the Five-Year Plans and the hardships endured by the masses. Another explanation stresses Stalin's determination to root out all possibility of opposition to his dictatorial power. Perhaps the most persuasive explanation was put forth by Merle Fainsod: 'The insecurity of the masses must be supplemented by the insecurity of the governing elite who surround the Supreme Dictator.' No official could be allowed to build up a strong following, lest he become strong enough to challenge Stalin. Under the Stalinist regime any citizen might well be disloyal, and thus the leader and his regime could be completely secure 'only if everyone is sufficiently terrorized to become incapable of acting independently.'

By late 1938, the terror by the state against its own people ended, probably because Stalin realized that if he continued on the path of violence the entire system might collapse. There was some evidence that party members had become so fearful that many refused to move into positions of authority. Whatever the reason, in April 1938 the Central Committee Plenum put out a warning against 'exaggerated vigilance' and placed the blame for the 'excesses' of the preceding five years on local party committees, and 'traitors' and Trotskyists who 'had wormed their way into the security organs.' Nevertheless, Stalin himself did not repudiate the terror, nor did he reduce the authority of the secret police.

8
Whither the Soviet Union?

Despite these domestic upheavals, the Soviet Union managed to transform itself into an industrial state of major proportions and an impressive military power within the short period of ten years. These achievements proved to be of critical importance when Nazi Germany launched its invasion of the Soviet Union on June 22, 1941, to be met by resistance so fierce that not only the Germans but also the rest of the world were surprised.

That resistance was all the more surprising because the first response to the invasion seemed to signal a quick and total collapse by the Russians, giving Hitler his greatest victory to date in World War II and assuring his dominance over the entire European continent. A major reason for Germany's early victories was that Stalin had given every indication that he had little to fear from the Nazis. True, he had ordered some increased spending on the military after the rise to power of Hitler in 1933, but at the same time he pursued domestic and foreign policies that suggested he did not suspect an attack by Germany. The purge of officers in the Red Army in 1937–8, many of them highly qualified strategists and administrators, greatly weakened the military services. Then, on 23 August 1939, Stalin signed a Non-Aggression Pact with the Nazis that gave Hitler a free hand to attack Poland. It also contained several secret provisions stipulating that after Poland's defeat, Eastern Europe would be divided between Germany and the Soviet Union. The agreement struck many people, among them a number of ardent radicals, as a horrendous betrayal of all that was decent.

Perhaps the most astonishing aspect of the negotiations with the Nazis was Stalin's conviction that Hitler intended to abide by the treaty permanently, or at least for several years. When Winston Churchill, the British prime minister who had led Britain in its war against Germany since June 1940, warned Stalin that Hitler's army was poised to attack the Soviet Union, the Bolshevik leader did not believe him, and made no effort to prepare for war. When it became clear that the Germans were indeed on the march, he apparently suffered a nervous breakdown and for about seven days was incapable of running the government or giving orders to military commanders.

The German army, superior in armor, strategy, tactics, and determination, was unstoppable. In addition, in the Ukraine, the Nazis were welcomed by many natives, who believed that life under the invaders would be preferable to rule by the Communists. In one month, the German army, under General von Bock's leadership, advanced five hundred miles; by mid-October, his troops stood at the gates of Moscow. By this time, the invaders had gained control over territories in which sixty million Soviet citizens (about 30 percent of the total) lived and which contained two-thirds of the country's oil reserves and three-fourths of its iron ore. In addition, the Russian army had suffered staggering losses: thousands of tanks, guns, and airplanes had been destroyed or captured, and the number of casualties endured during the first four months of the war ran to over three million.

In the meantime, Stalin had recovered, resumed his duties as leader of the country, and, surprisingly, turned out to be extraordinarily effective in rousing the nation for the war effort and in guiding the military to put up a robust defense. He quickly understood that his major task was to appeal to the patriotism of the people; he did not hesitate to invoke many of the symbols of traditional Russian nationalism, which had long been derided by the Communists. Nor did he hesitate to dismiss civilian or military officials incapable of coping with the endless crises they confronted. It did not take the Russian people long to respond positively to his appeals to make sacrifices to save their homeland. The invaders played right into Stalin's hands. Instead of taking advantage of the masses' discontents under Communism, the Germans treated the natives in the conquered territories as *Untermenschen* (subhumans). In short order, Hitler's army faced millions of hostile people who went to great lengths—including extensive guerrilla warfare—to hamper the invaders.

The tide began definitively to turn against the German army in September 1942, when Hitler's troops failed to capture Stalingrad, the city on the Volga that the Führer was determined to capture, because he assumed that the capture of the city with that name would be a fatal blow to the country. However, the Russian troops fought gallantly and after a successful counterattack, surrounded the German army, which had no choice but to capitulate in February 1943. Five months later, in July 1943, the Russians defeated the enemy in a now-famous battle near Kursk (in southwest Russia). It was the first time that Soviet troops had beaten the Germans in what had come to be known as a specialty of German commanders: 'mobile warfare.' One reason for the Russian success was that the Soviet Union had received a considerable amount of advanced equipment from Great Britain and the United States. After this victory, Russian troops moved quickly westward, but they were ordered to halt their offensive in the summer of 1944, when not far from Warsaw, Poland's capital. Stalin, it has been suggested, wanted to give the Germans ample time to deliver a serious blow at the Polish Home Army, which had fought on the side of the Russians but made clear its distaste for Communism. Stalin directed his forces to capture Romania and Hungary instead, guaranteeing that these two countries would be satellites of the Soviet Union. Eventually, the Russian troops resumed their march through Poland into Germany. When the war ended, in May 1945, the Soviet army was entrenched in six East European countries, as well as East Germany.

Thus, the sphere of socialism was vastly expanded, leading many people to believe that the Bolsheviks' original dream of world revolution was at last within reach. However, within a few years, it became clear that the Eastern European countries would not easily succumb to Russian domination. Moreover, the Soviet Union had paid a heavy price for the victory over the German invader. A few statistics will suffice to indicate the country's losses between 1941 and 1942: agricultural production declined from 95.5 million tons to 30 million tons, and the number of cattle declined by 50 percent. Over the entire war, famine and Nazi brutality toward Russians are estimated to have caused the death of well over twelve million people; in addition, some eight million people died as a result of enemy military action.

In view of these statistics, it is remarkable that within a few years of the end of World War II, the Soviet Union became one of the two great powers in the world, considered by some to approach the strength of the United States. Most notably, the Soviet army vastly extended the reach of Communism: Communist governments were established in Poland, Czechoslovakia, Romania, Hungary, Yugoslavia, Albania, and East Germany. Although there were indications that the people of these countries chafed under the new regime—rebellions broke out against the new system of rule in East Germany in 1953, in Hungary in 1956, and in Czechoslovakia in 1968—all generally remained subservient to the government in Moscow. In 1949, the Soviet Union became a nuclear power, vastly increasing its influence in international affairs. Over the next three decades, the Communists became rivals of the West in many parts of the world and succeeded in establishing footholds in the Middle East, Africa, and even Latin

America. China had undergone its own Communist revolution in 1949 and also became an adversary of the West, although its relations with the Soviet Union did not remain cordial for long.

Relations between the Soviet Union and the West cooled to such an extent that the years from 1946 to the early 1990s came to be known as the era of the Cold War, which for the most part was confined to economic, political, and military rivalries between the Communist and capitalist blocs. Actually, the two worlds never overcame the suspicions each harbored of the other during the days of close collaboration in the war against Nazi Germany. The Communists were enraged at the failure of the West to relieve the Soviet army in 1942 and 1943 by opening a second front against Germany. Actually, the West was militarily too weak to do so. On the other hand, political leaders in the West, most notably Winston Churchill, feared that the Soviet Union's control over Eastern Europe was only a prelude to attempts to spread socialism to Europe and eventually the rest of the world, a fear harking back to the earliest period of the Bolshevik seizure of power in 1917. The 'official' beginning of the Cold War is generally believed to have been Churchill's famous speech, made in Fulton, Missouri, in March 1946, in which he asserted that 'an iron curtain has descended across the continent [stretching] from Stettin in the Baltic to Trieste in the Adriatic,' and urged cooperation between the United States and Europe to nip in the bud any 'temptation to ambition or adventure,' a clear reference to what he believed to be the expansionist intentions of Stalin.

Basically, the Cold War amounted to a fierce rivalry between the West and the Soviet Union, but once, in October 1962, the relations between the two sides took a dangerous turn, threatening to lead to a military conflict in which both sides considered using nuclear weapons. Nikita Khrushchev, then the leader of the Soviet Union, had decided that John F. Kennedy, the American president, was a young, inexperienced head of state, who would not dare to respond forcefully to a provocative move by the Soviet Union. Resentful of the Americans having bases in Turkey, within easy striking distance of the Soviet Union, Khrushchev decided to establish bases in Cuba, fifty miles from the United States. When American planes spotted the new facilities, Kennedy became alarmed; after considering an air strike he imposed a blockade, called a 'quarantine,' on Soviet ships carrying military supplies to Cuba. For a few days, the two sides were on the brink of war, but after a series of back-channel negotiations, Khrushchev abandoned his plans to place nuclear weapons in Cuba. In return, Kennedy agreed never to attack Cuba and to dismantle military bases in Turkey and Italy from which missiles could be fired at the Communist bloc countries. The Cold War continued for about another three decades, but both sides avoided provocations that could lead to military conflict.

By this time, the Soviet Union had completed more than a decade of what might be called post-Stalinist Communism. Stalin had died early in March 1953, after a series of bizarre events that seemed to suggest that the country was on the verge of another outbreak of state terror similar to the bloodletting of the years between 1936 and 1938. Early in 1953, the authorities announced that a group of doctors, most clearly Jewish, had made plans to murder, by medical means, a large number of people who occupied leading positions in the government. The agencies charged with protecting the nation's leaders and safeguarding the socialist state were accused of incompetence in not detecting the growing danger. This seemed to be an ominous signal that a new wave of terror from above was being planned. It is now widely believed that this was prevented by Stalin's unexpected death on 5 March. In fact, rumors widely circulated that he had been murdered. The evidence in support of that charge was not convincing. Stalin was seventy-three years old and it was known that he had suffered a stroke some years earlier. In 1955, N. S. Khrushchev, for many years a major figure in Stalin's administration, had seized control of the government and immediately took steps to prevent a recurrence of mass terror. He went so far as to have Lavrenti Beria, Stalin's henchman in the terror of the 1930s, shot without trial.

The collapse of the Soviet Union

As a nuclear power, the Soviet Union could rattle its saber, but the government's focus on worldwide influence was bound to be short-lived. True, the people of the Soviet Union took pride in the country's military and diplomatic achievements, yet at the same time many citizens became increasingly critical of domestic developments. The standard of living of the vast majority of the people, very low to begin with, lagged far behind that of other industrialized countries. From the mid-1960s, labor productivity in the Soviet Union was significantly lower than that of capitalist America and the welfare states of Europe. For example, in the period from 1951 to 1965, the rate of increase in productivity amounted to between 40 and 50 percent of that of the American workers. In 1963, miners in the United States produced an average of 14 tons of coal per day, whereas their Soviet counterparts produced 2.1 tons per day, even though the level of mechanization was about the same. About one-fifth of what is referred to as the 'caloric intake' of the Soviet people had to be imported—this, at a time of growing budget deficits. In a poll of 1991, two-thirds of the people reported that the *per capita* income of their families was less than 125 rubles a month—about two hundred dollars at the official rate of exchange, but more like twenty dollars on the free market. Health services were in dreadful condition, as is demonstrated by a decline in longevity between 1959 and 1979, from 69.3 years to 67.7 years. Many people in the Soviet Union concluded that the country's economic system was on the wrong track. Western economists—and in time a growing number of Soviet economists—attributed these dismal statistics to the rigid controls from above, the absence of adequate incentives for hard work, and the prevalence of corruption at every level of society.

It was now also beyond doubt that the economic and social egalitarianism that the founders of Communism had promised was not part of Soviet reality. There were wide differences in income for various categories of workers, and those at the top of the social hierarchy lived far better than the masses. A joke circulating in the 1970s nicely captures the public attitude toward the country's upper classes and their disrespect for Communist principles. Leonid Brezhnev, the General Secretary of the party from 1967 until 1982, took his aging mother on a tour of the lavish country homes where he kept his cars and lived luxuriously. She remained silent until the frustrated Brezhnev finally asked her point blank what she thought of all his comforts. 'It's very nice,' she responded, 'but what will happen when the Communists come back to power?'

That did not happen. Instead, the Communist system of rule collapsed shortly after M. S. Gorbachev, who acceded to power as General Secretary in 1985, began to introduce major political and economic reforms. Few senior officials expected the fifty-four-year-old Gorbachev, who had held important positions in the Communist Party for some fifteen years, to lead the country in a fundamentally new direction. He was, as the British historian Robert Service put it, 'a brilliant dissimulator;' in public he toed the party line, but in private conversations with his family and closest friends he had expressed, ever since his days as a student at Moscow State University (from 1950 to 1955), dissatisfaction with conditions in his country, although he had only the vaguest notion of how to improve matters.

Soon after assuming the office of General Secretary, Gorbachev launched a reform program, but his first effort was ill-advised and unsuccessful. He initiated a campaign against alcoholism, which had become a public health hazard seriously affecting labor productivity; it remains a problem even now, in 2013. The government reduced the output of liquor and restricted its sale, but many people refused to do without their favorite drinks and resorted to using industrial products such as methylated spirits and antifreeze to produce homemade substitutes. Both were of inferior quality and, more important, harmful. Within three years, the government quietly dropped the campaign.

Gorbachev's cultural and political reforms were more widely appreciated and more enduring. In 1986, he adopted the policy of *glasnost*, a hazy term that literally meant 'publicity' or 'openness,' but which eventually acquired a variety of meanings. The General Secretary seems to have had in mind little more than that the government would be more forthcoming in explaining its conduct of national affairs. Within short order, that vague program was abandoned in favor of the dissemination of information and opinions on a wide range of issues. More importantly, within two years the press and television were permitted to air subjects that had been officially kept under wraps for decades. Stalinist terror, censorship, the degradation of the environment, corruption, crime, the failings of the health services, and the intrigues at the highest levels of authority were freely discussed. Works of fiction and scholarly books on sensitive subjects that had been proscribed because they did not adhere to the party line were published and widely read by the educated classes, who harbored strong misgivings about the government's conduct of affairs. They also sensed that economically and socially the country lagged far behind Western democracies.

Glasnost was part of a larger reform that Gorbachev had conceived, which he dubbed *perestroika* (reconstruction). Again, he did not clearly define the notion; all he said when he first used the word in 1985 was, 'Obviously, we all must undergo reconstruction, all of us. ... Everyone must adopt new approaches and understand that no other path is available to us.' Perestroika was a watchword, a catch-all for the transformation of Soviet society.

Gorbachev considered himself a dedicated Marxist; he wanted
to reform the Soviet Union, but he did not intend to abandon
the fundamental principles that had inspired the creation of the
socialist order in 1917.

His commitment to Marxist doctrines made it impossible
for him to cope effectively with the nation's economic problems, which continued to worsen at an alarming pace. Within
one year, 1990, the net national product declined by 9 percent.
Prices rose precipitately, and some staple products, such as milk,
tea, coffee, and soap, became hard to find. In numerous districts,
the authorities introduced rationing. The central government
tried various reforms to stimulate the economy, but none worked.
Several leading economists recommended the abandonment by
the government of central control over the system; it seems that
Gorbachev showed interest in this radical step, but in the end could
not propose a measure that would undermine the socialist order.

In the political sphere, Gorbachev was bolder. He established
a series of institutions that seemed to be the bedrock of a democratic order; the new political structure gave the people a real
voice in national affairs. A Congress of People's Deputies, consisting of 2,250 members, was elected and was to meet annually,
serving as a check on the executive part of the government. The
congress elected a Supreme Soviet of fifty-four, which met twice
a year and served as a legislature operating more or less like Western parliaments. Gorbachev hoped this structure would enable
the country to remain loyal to the principles of Marxism.

These efforts at reform were laudable in many respects, but
they failed to achieve their purpose to modernize and revital-
ize the Soviet Union. Gorbachev seems not to have been familiar with a cardinal rule of politics, first enunciated by Alexis
de Tocqueville, 'that the most dangerous moment for a bad
government is generally that in which it sets about reform.' It
did not occur to the General Secretary that, in Soviet society

and countries that had adopted the Soviet system of rule, his reforms might unleash a chain reaction of demands for more freedom and better economic conditions that he would not be able to control. He was especially surprised that his proposals triggered protest movements among the national minorities and in Eastern Europe, movements that played a major role in the eventual breakup of the Soviet Union. The entire institution of government had become so inefficient and corrupt that a large percentage of the people would accept nothing less than a new economic and political system. To everyone's astonishment, in 1991 the Soviet Empire crumbled altogether, and with less bloodshed than in 1917, when the tsarist Empire had collapsed. Eastern European countries abandoned Communism and declared their full independence. More astonishing, the Soviet Union disintegrated into fifteen separate states, the former constituent republics. The Russian Federation, the largest state to emerge from the former Soviet Union, turned to capitalism and democracy after Gorbachev's removal from office, although the new economic and political systems bear little resemblance to the capitalist democracies of the West.

Only a minority of those who had lived under the Soviet system of rule mourned the end of the dreams of John Reed and Vladimir Lenin. In some respects, the dreams of 1917 were noble, and it is easy to see why so many people were captivated by them, but they were also highly unrealistic, especially in a country as poor and politically undeveloped as Russia. That the experiment of the Russian Revolution failed so quickly is not surprising. By 1945, the Soviet Union had been transformed into what appeared to be a mighty empire, but it was short-lived, lasting a mere seventy-four years, not comparable in durability to other great empires, most notably the Roman, Spanish, and British. In the final analysis, the Soviet Empire collapsed because it was based on utopian ideals, and not even men with pure and noble souls could have realized them. Neither Lenin nor most of his successors could be regarded as men of virtue; they were all too willing to resort to the most ruthless means to realize their dreams, but even then, they could not create the kind of society they considered ideal.

Afterword

The Soviet experiment in creating a socialist society failed after only a few decades, but its legacy in Russia has been far more enduring and pernicious than anticipated. Boris N. Yeltsin, the first President of the Russian Federation—as the country was known after it separated from fourteen regions that had gained independence—promised to transform the new state into a democracy in which private ownership of property would be permitted. However, the Russian Federation lacked deeply rooted traditions of popular government, as well as the legal and economic institutions that are the backbone of capitalism, and, perhaps, most importantly, it lacked cadres of citizens familiar with the principles and practices of democracy. None of the government's plans to move from authoritarian collectivism to popular rule and free enterprise proved to be effective.

President Yeltsin was too erratic to bring about the changes he promised when he assumed the leadership of the Russian Federation. He flitted from enthusiasm for democratic institutions to a conviction that the Russian people needed and wanted a strong leader. He became increasingly authoritarian and soon viewed himself as the 'father of the nation,' prompting many people to refer to him as 'Tsar Boris,' a title that seemed to appeal to him. He was also a troubled man, who suffered from deep depressions, during which he would disappear from public view for weeks at a time. To add to his woes, in the mid-1990s he was struck down by several heart attacks. Under the circumstances, none of his promised reforms were realized, and the economy, in dreadful condition in the 1980s, continued to decline at an alarming pace. True, a substantial portion of the economy was privatized, but the main beneficiaries were not the people at large but a small group of oligarchs who exercised enormous influence over government policy.

After a series of intense political conflicts with various groups that opposed his rule, Yeltsin—by then very ill—resigned on 31 December 1999. One of his last official actions was to appoint Vladimir Putin, who had served as Prime Minister for about five months, as acting president. It was widely assumed that Yeltsin had turned to Putin because he had been assured that the new government would not investigate charges of corruption against Yeltsin's family and entourage.

Putin's assumption of power as President, following an election early in 2000 that he won easily, did not augur well for democracy in Russia. An unknown bureaucrat before 1999, who had spent most of his adult life working for the Soviet security services, he never lost his devotion to the Communist regime. In April 2007, he made this clear when he said that 'we should acknowledge that the collapse of the Soviet Union was a major geopolitical disaster for the country.'

In some respects, Putin turned out to be an effective ruler; he instituted policies that restored political stability and economic progress. The standard of living in the Russian Federation still lags far behind that of Western democracies, but conditions have improved markedly since the chaotic 1980s and 1990s. However, the political system in the Federation still bears many of the marks of the autocratic regime under Communism. An American diplomatic cable that was illegally leaked to the press in 2010 noted that corruption was so widespread that the country should be considered a 'virtual mafia state.' An article in *The New York Times* of 16 May 2013 indicated how little respect the government has for the rights of its citizens. It reported that the authorities in Moscow rejected a bid by gay rights advocates to hold a parade because it could 'undermine a campaign to instill patriotic values in the city's youths.' It seems clear that the view prevalent in ruling circles in the Soviet Union, that the government has the right to control its citizens' values and private conduct, has not been abandoned.

Timeline

1907	February 7: Opening of Second Duma
	June 3: Dissolution of Second Duma; enactment of new, restrictive electoral laws
1914	July 19 (commonly noted as August 1 in the Gregorian calendar): Germany declares war on Russia
	Late August: Russian army suffers defeat in East Prussia
1915	June–July: Progressive Bloc formed in Duma
	Russian troops badly defeated by German army
1916	November 1: Miliukov suggests treason committed by senior officials
	December 16: Murder of Rasputin
1917	February 14: Anti-government demonstrations begin in Petrograd
	February 23: Demonstrations on Women's Day
	February 24–25: Increase in Petrograd demonstrations
	February 27: Soldiers refuse to fire on demonstrators
	March 2: Formation of Provisional Government: Tsar Nicholas abdicates
	March 4: Provisional Government dismisses all governors and their deputies
	April 3: Lenin arrives in Petrograd from Switzerland
	May 4: Trotsky arrives in Russia
	May 5: Kerensky appointed Minister of War
	June 3–5: Meeting of First All-Russian Congress of Soviets of Workers' and Soldiers' Deputies
	June 16: Russian military offensive begins

July 3–5: July Days – massive demonstrations against government

July 5: Russian offensive collapses in face of German counteroffensive

July 8: Kerensky appointed Prime Minister

August 22–25: Moscow State Conference

August 27–31: Kornilov Affair

September 25: Trotsky elected Chairman of Petrograd Soviet

October 24: Kerensky orders closing of Bolshevik newspapers

October 25–26: Bolsheviks seize power

October 26: Second Congress of Soviets adopts decrees on land, peace and on establishment of new government known as Council of People's Commissars

December 7: Creation of Cheka

1918	January 5–6: Constituent Assembly meets; dispersed by Bolsheviks
	March 1: Russia signs peace treaty with Germany
	March 9: Foreign intervention in Russia begins
	Spring: Civil War begins
	June: Introduction of War Communism
	July 16–17: Tsar Nicholas II and family executed in Ekaterinburg
	August 30: Attempted assassination of Lenin
1919	Late that year Bolsheviks defeat opponents in Civil War
1920	May: Russia at war with Poland

1921	March 2: Kronstadt rebellion
	March: Introduction of New Economic Policy
1922	Country officially designated as Union of Soviet Socialist Republic
1924	January: Lenin dies
1924–28	Struggle for succession to Lenin
1928	Stalin becomes Supreme Leader
	Introduction of Five-Year Plan; collectivization of peasants' farms
1934	December 1: Murder of S. M. Kirov; beginning of State Terror
1937	Purge of military officers
1940	Murder of Trotsky in Mexico
1941	June 22: Nazi Germany invades Russia
1943	July: Soviet victory at Stalingrad
1945	Soviet Union emerges from World War II as major world power
1946–early 1990s	Cold War
1953	March 5: Stalin dies
1962	October 14–28: Cuban Missile Crisis
1985	M. Gorbachev appointed Secretary-General of Communist Party; introduces series of reforms
1991	Collapse of Soviet Union; end of Cold War

Bibliography

Ascher, Abraham *P. A. Stolypin: The Struggle for Stability in Late Imperial Russia*. Stanford, CA, 2001

_____ 'Russian Marxism and the German Revolution, 1917–1920,' *Archiv für Sozialgeschichte*, VI-VII (1966–67), pp. 391–437.

_____ 'The Kornilov Affair,' *Russian Review*, 12, no. 4*1953), pp. 235–52.

_____ *The Russian Revolution of 1905*, 2 vols. Stanford, CA, 1988–92.

Avrich, P. *Kronstadt 1921*. Princeton, 1970.

_____ *The Russian Anarchists*, Princeton, 1967.

Bonnell, Victoria E. *Roots of Rebellion*. Berkeley, 1983.

Bradley, Joseph. *Muzhik and Muscovite: Urbanization in Late Imperial Russia*. Berkeley, CA, 1985.

Browder, Robert Paul and Aleksandr Fyodorovich Kerensky. *The Russian Provisional Government, 1917: Documents*. Stanford, CA, 1961.

Brown, Archie *The Gorbachev Factor*. Oxford, 1997.

Burbank, Jane *Intelligentsia and Revolution: Russian Views of Bolshevism, 1917–1922*. New York, 1986.

Bushnell, John. *Mutiny amid Repression: Russian Soldiers in the Revolution of 1905–06*. Bloomington, IN, 1985

Carr, Edward Hallett. *The Bolshevik Revolution, 1917–1923*. 3 vols. New York, 1951–61.

Chamberlin, William H. *The Russian Revolution, 1917–1921.* 2 vols. New York, 1960.

Chernov, Victor. *The Great Russian Revolution.* New Haven, 1926.

Cohen, Stephen F. *Bukharin and the Bolshevik Revolution.* New York, 1971.

Conquest, Robert. *The Great Terror: A Reassessment.* New York, 1990.

Denikin Anton I. *The Russian Turmoil: Memoirs Military, Social and Political.* London, 1922.

Deutscher, Isaac *Prophet Outcast: Trotsky, 1929–1940.* New York, 1959.

_____ *Prophet Unarmed: Trotsky, 1921–1929.* New York, 1959.

_____ *The Prophet Armed: Trotsky, 1978–1921.* New York, 1954.

Emmons, Terence. 'Russian Banquet Campaign,' *California Slavic Studies.* 10(1977), pp. 45–86

Engelstein, Laura. *Moscow, 1905.* Stanford, CA, 1982.

Fainsod, Merle. *How Russia is Ruled,* rev. edn. Cambridge, MA, 1963.

Figes, Orlando. *A People's Tragedy.* New York, 1997.

Fitzpatrick, Sheila. *Everyday Stalinism: Ordinary Life in Extraordinary Times: Russia in the 1930s.* New York, 1999.

_____ *The Russian Revolution.* 2nd edn. Oxford, 1994.

Frankel, Edith R., Jonathan Frankel and Baruch Knei-Paz, eds., *Revolution in Russia: Reassessments of 1917.* Cambridge, UK, 1992.

Frankel, Jonathan. *Prophesy and Politics: Socialism, Nationalism, and the Russian Jews, 1862–1917.* Cambridge, UK, 1981.

Galai, Shmuel. *The Liberation Movement in Russia, 1900–1905.* Cambridge, 1973.

Galili, Ziva. *The Menshevik Leaders in the Russian Revolution: Social Realities and Political Strategies.* Princeton, 1989.

Getzler, Israel. *Martov: A Political Biography of a Russian Social Democrat.* Cambridge, 1964.

_____ *Kronstadt 1917–1921: The Fate of Soviet Democracy.* Cambridge, UK, 2002.

_____ *Nikolai Sukhanov: Chronicler of the Russian Revolution.* London, 2002.

Goldman, Marshall I. *USSR in Crisis: The Failure of an Economic System.* New York, 1983.

Haimson, Leopold H. *The Russian Marxists and the Origins of Bolshevism.* Cambridge, MA, 1955.

_____ 'The Problem of Social Stability in Urban Russia,' *Slavic Review* 23, no. 4(1964), 619–42; 24, no. 1(1965), 1–23.

Hasegawa, Tsuyoshi. *The February Revolution: Petrograd 1917.* Seattle, 1981.

Hosking, Geoffrey. *The Awakening of the Soviet Union.* Cambridge, MA, 1991.

_____ *The First Socialist Society: A History of the Soviet Union from Within.* Cambridge, MA, 1993.

_____ *The Russian Constitutional Experiment: Government and Duma, 1907–1914.* Cambridge, 1973.

Katkov, George *Russia 1917: The Kornilov Affair: Kerensky and the Break-up of the Russian Army.* London, 1980.

Keep, John H.L. *The Rise of Social Democracy in Russia.* Oxford, 1965.

_____ *The Russian Revolution: A Study in Mass Mobilization.* New York, 1976.

Kennan, George. *Soviet-American Relations in 1917–1920.* Princeton, 1956, 1958.

Kotkin, Stephen. *Magnetic Mountain: Stalinism as a Civilization.* Berkeley, 1995.

Laqueur, Walter. *The Dream that Failed: Reflections on the Soviet Union.* New York, 1996.

_____ *The Fate of the Revolution; Interpretations of Soviet History from 1917 to the Present.* New York, 1987.

Legett, George. *The Cheka: Lenin's Political Police.* New York, 1987.

Lenin, V. I. *Collected Works.* 45 vols. Moscow, 1960–70.

Lewin, Moshe. *Russian Peasants and Soviet Power: A Study of Collectivization.* New York, 1975.

Lieven, Dominic C.B. *Nicholas II: Twilight of the Empire*: New York, 1994.

_____ *Russia and the Origins of the First World War.* New York, 1983.

Manning, Roberta T. *The Crisis of the Old Order in Russia.* Princeton, 1982.

Miller, Margaret S. *The Economic Development of Russia, 1905–1914*, 2nd edn. London, 1967.

Nove, Alec. *An Economic History of the USSR*, 3rd edn. London, 1990.

Pipes, Richard E. *The Formation of the Soviet Union: Communism and Nationalism, 1917–1923.* Cambridge, MA, 1964.

_____ *Russia under the Bolshevik Regime.* New York, 1994.

_____ *The Russian Revolution.* New York, 1991.

Rabinowitch, Alexander. *Bolsheviks Come to Power: the Revolution of 1917 in Petrograd.* New York, 1976.

_____ *Bolsheviks in Power: the First Year of Soviet Rule in Petrograd.* Bloomington, IN, 2007.

_____ *Prelude to Revolution: the Petrograd Bolsheviks and the July 1917 Uprising.* Bloomington, IN, 1991.

Radkey, Oliver H. *The Agrarian Foes of Bolshevism: Promise and Default of the Russian Socialist Revolution, February to October 1917.* New York, 1958.

_____ *The Sickle under the Hammer: The Russian Socialist Revolutionaries in the Early Months of Soviet Rule.* New York, 1964.

Raeff, Marc *Political Ideas and Institutions in Imperial Russia.* Boulder, 1994.

Reed, John *Ten Days that Shook the World.* New York, 1919.

Rimlinger, Gaston V. 'Autocracy and the Factory Order in Early Russian Industrialization,' *Journal of Economic History*, 1960, no. 1, pp. 67–92.

_____ 'The Management of Labor Protests in Tsarist Russia: 1870–1905' *International Review of Social History*, 5(1960), part 2, pp. 226–48.

Robbins, Richard G. *The Tsar's Viceroy.* Ithaca, 1987.

Robinson, Geroid T.R. *Rural Russia under the Old Regime.* New York, 1932.

Rogger, Hans *Russia in the Age of Modernization and Revolution.* London and New York, 1983.

Rosenberg, William *Liberals in the Russian Revolution: The Constitutional Democratic Party, 1917–1921.*

Saunders, D. *Russia in the Age of Reaction and Reform, 1801–1881.* London and New York, 1992.

Schapiro, Leonard. *The Communist Party of the Soviet Union.* London, 1960.

_____ *The Origins of the Communist Autocracy.* London, 1955.

_____ *Totalitarianism.* London, 1972.

Service, Robert. *A History of Twentieth-Century Russia.* Cambridge, MA, 1997.

_____ *Lenin.* 3 vols. London, 1985–95.

Shevtsova, Lilia *Russia Lost in Transition: The Yeltsin and Putin Legacies.* Washington, D.C., 2007.

Smele, Jonathan D. *Civil War in Siberia: the anti-Bolshevik Movement of Admiral Kolchak, 1918–1920.* Cambridge, 1996.

_____ (ed.) *Russian Revolution and Civil War: an Annotated Bibliography.* London, 2003.

Stalin, J.V. *Works*. 15 vols. Moscow, 1954

Stites, Richard *Revolutionary Dreams: Utopian Visions and Experimental Life in the Russian Revolution*. New York, 1989.

Stockdale, Melissa K. *Paul Miliukov and the Quest for a Liberal Russia, 1880–1918*. Ithaca, 1996.

Strakhovsky, Leonid I. 'Was there a Kornilov Rebellion? – A Re-appraisal of the Evidence,' *The Slavonic and East European Review*, XXXIII (June 1955), 372–95.

Suhr, Gerald D. *1905 in St. Petersburg: Labor, Society and Revolution*. Stanford, CA, 1989.

Sukhanov, Nikollai N. *The Russian Revolution 1917: Eyewitness Account*. 2.vols. Edited, abridged and translated by Joel Carmichael. 2 vols. New York, 1962.

Trotsky, L. D. *History of the Russian Revolution*, tr. Max Eastman. New York, 1936.

_____ *My Life: An Attempt at an Autobiography*. New York, 1930.

Tucker, Robert C. *Stalin as a Revolutionary, 1879–1929*. New York, 1975.

_____ *Stalin in Power: The Revolution from Above, 1928–1941*. New York, 1990.

Ulam, Adam *Expansion and Coexistence: The History of Soviet Foreign Policy, 1917–67*. New York, 1968.

_____ *The Bolsheviks: The Intellectual and Political History of the Triumph of Communism in Russia*. New York, 1965.

_____ *Stalin: The Man and His Era*. Boston, 1987.

Venturi, Franco *Roots of Revolution: A History of the Populist and Socialist Movements in Nineteenth-Century Russia*. New York, 1960.

Von Laue, Theodore H. *Sergei Witte and the Industrialization of Russia*. New York, 1963.

Wade, Rex A. *Red Guards and Workers' Militias*. Stanford, CA, 1984.

_____ *The Russian Revolution, 1917*, 2nd edn Cambridge, 2005.

_____ *The Russian Search for Peace, February–October 1917*. Stanford, CA, 1969.

White, James D. 'The Kornilov Affair: A Study in Counter Revolution,' *Soviet Studies* 20, no. 2 (1968–69), 18 7–205.

White, John A., *The Diplomacy of the Russo-Japanese War*, New York, Princeton, N.J., 1964

Wildman, Allan K. *The End of the Russian Imperial Army: the Old Army and the Soldier' Revolt (March–April 1917)*, Princeton, 1980.

_____ *The End of the Russian Imperial Army. The Road to Soviet Power and Peace*. Princeton, 1987.

Williams, Harold *Russia of the Russians*. New York, 1918.

Wolfe, Bertram D. *Three Who Made a Revolution*. New York, 1948.

Wortman, Richard *The Crisis of Russian Populism*. Cambridge, UK, 1967.

_____ *Scenarios of Power: Myth and Ceremony in Russian Monarchy*. Vol. 2. Princeton, 2000.

Wynn, Charters. *Workers, Strikers, and Pogroms*. Princeton, 1992.

Zelnik, Reginald E. *Labor and Society in Tsarist Russia: the Factory Workers of St. Petersburg, 1855–1870*. Stanford, CA, 1971.

_____ *Law and Disorder in the Narova River. The Kreenholm Strike of 1872*. Berkely and Los Angeles, CA, 1995.

Zeman, Zbynek and W. B. Scharlau *Merchant of Revolution*: Alexander Helphand, 1867-1924. Oxford, 1965.

Index